I struggle with prayer the way tha[...]
prayer. And yet Leslie Leyland Fiel[...]
what she calls "a new place that is not far or hard to g[...]
With gentleness, grace, and exquisite language, Leslie is
the guide who is leading me, and you, to the One who is
near.

> **MARGOT STARBUCK,** author of *Small Things with Great Love*

Leslie Leyland Fields has provided a journey through the Psalms
engaging your heart, mind, body, and soul. Slow down and
process these ancient words. Your life will be richer for the
journey.

> **CHRIS FABRY,** author, host of *Chris Fabry Live*

Leslie Leyland Fields has displayed her extraordinary gifts as
a writer in a growing list of publications. In *Nearing a Far
God* she turns to the inspired poetry of the Psalms. Here
she encourages us, and shows us how, to bring our whole
selves to the Psalms and put them before God. She does that
very thing in the book, moving from moments in her own
life into the rich texts of the Psalms. Sunday school classes,
Bible study groups, and individuals will find *Nearing a Far
God* to be a wonderful guide into a deep reading of the
Psalms, where they may confidently expect to be engaged
by God.

> **BEN C. OLLENBURGER, PhD,** emeritus professor,
> author of *God the Creator*

What is prayer—really? What is prayer when we let it and our lives be the complicated messes they are? And why wouldn't our emotions—shamed by a previous generation of evangelicals—be part of our prayers? Leslie Leyland Fields demonstrates fierce and authentic praying as she reframes old, limited notions of prayer. Fields avoids easy how-to steps or simple answers and teaches us how to integrate praying the Psalms with being richly and deeply human.

CYNTHIA BEACH, author of *The Surface of Water*

Practical, theologically informed, rich with insight, these personal encounters with the Psalms give readers an imaginative, life-giving way to bring these ancient prayers into the very heart of the lives we live now. Grounded in scenes from her own remarkable life, Leslie leads us step by step through a process of claiming each psalm, making it our own, uniting our cries for help and exuberant thanksgivings to those of all who have prayed them over centuries. This book offers a new way of understanding the Bible as a living word: It lives in those who enter it with faith, hope, and all the particulars of our messy lives, letting it shape our prayers and listening for the voice that calls us by name.

MARILYN McENTYRE, PhD, author of *Caring for Words in a Culture of Lies* and *Word by Word*

I've long been an admirer of Leslie Leyland Fields, her lyrical prose, and her wisdom. This beautiful, honest book does not disappoint. What sets *Nearing a Far God* apart is Fields's masterful ability to blend the timeless wisdom of the Psalms with the practical realities of our lives today. Her words are a source of comfort for those in times of sorrow and a celebration for those experiencing moments of joy. This book is a gentle, trustworthy guide for those yearning to draw nearer to God.

JENNIFER DUKES LEE, author of *Growing Slow* and *It's All Under Control*

Nearing
a Far God

praying
the psalms
with our
whole
selves

Leslie
Leyland
Fields

NavPress

A NavPress resource published in alliance
with Tyndale House Publishers

NavPress.com

The Team:
David Zimmerman, Publisher; Caitlyn Carlson, Senior Editor; Caleb Sjogren, Copy Editor; Olivia Eldredge, Operations Manager; Dean Renninger, Designer

To all the brave, creative people in my writing community
and to the wondrous Story Leaders,
who prayed and cheered me through these pages.
Here our stories find their true ending.

contents

introduction

I was eight or nine the first time I prayed.

"Come, everyone—we're going into the front room," my mother called out to me and five siblings. I don't remember what I was doing—maybe playing marbles with my brother on the red-and-blue patterned carpet. It was summer, warm. All six of us were dressed in our hand-me-downs: striped cotton jerseys, baggy cotton shorts.

I looked at my mother's face, puzzled. We came right away; we never questioned her authority. She had directed us through the long, arduous process of transforming this rambling two-hundred-year-old New Hampshire house back to its colonial integrity. But this didn't sound like another job.

We spread out nervously, some on the couch, some in the hard-backed rocking chairs, all of us silent, curious. She began: "Remember that family that looked at the house a few days ago?"

By this point, we paid little attention to the stream of people strolling through our house. The house had been for sale for at least a year, maybe two.

"We're going to bow our heads and think as hard as we can about them buying the house." There was tension in my mother's voice. "Just send out those positive thoughts."

We had never done this before. What was it? Was this prayer? And why would God—or the universe or whatever we were praying to—why would he or she or it listen to six ragged children and their exhausted mother? But I dutifully bowed my head and squinched my eyes and covered my face with my hands. *Let the house sell! Let those people buy the house!* I chanted silently over and over, imagining the words pressing out through my brain and into the clouds and beyond.

My brothers and sisters were quiet as well. I peeked up through a crack in my fingers. Their heads were on their knees or in their laps. Where were their words going? Were we all sending our thoughts into the minds of the other family? Maybe it would work.

These were the days of Norman Vincent Peale and positive thinking. I had seen his book in our house but didn't know anything beyond the optimism of the title.

That family didn't buy the house, despite our ardent appeals to the universe. The lesson I took from that day was not that prayer didn't work, but that prayer was for desperate people. And that God, or whomever we were praying to, was too far away to hear us or too busy to help.

I still believe that prayer is for desperate people. But I have come to believe something different about God: that God, even when he feels far away, is closer than we know. And he longs for us to draw near.

I will be honest—I have resisted such closeness. Despite speaking and teaching and even praying in churches for years, I'm still a novice at prayer.

My friend Roberta doesn't know this about me. I'm on the phone with her now. Over the years, she has lost three children out of six, one by one. "I can hardly pray anymore," she tells me. Her voice is flat. "God doesn't want to hear from me. Why would he take my kids away?"

In the face of such vast suffering, I feel ignorant and helpless. "I'm so sorry, Roberta. I understand," I say. I'm lying. What do I know of loss like this? "Ummm, I'll pray for you." My words are a reflex. I don't know what else to say.

"I know you pray a lot," she says. "You pray to God like he's right there with you."

I wince. I want to set her right, but she is old and we're on the phone, and I don't want to start an argument or sound falsely humble. If only she knew that any humility I feel is closer to humiliation. Yes, I know how to speak pious words, especially with a mic at my throat—but I have objections and doubts. I'm well versed in theology, but it often stays stuck in my head. Sometimes I forget God is here. I don't always believe God wants to hear from me. I struggle to believe I'm accepted and forgiven. My heart goes cold and numb way too often. Sometimes I just want to run my own life.

Do you feel that way too? You likely have more to add to this list of objections and struggles. Maybe God feels far away, even oblivious to your existence. Maybe you've never prayed because you're not sure God is even there. Or maybe you believe he is there, but you're sure he isn't listening. Maybe you've lived a messy life, and you're pretty sure no God could be interested in you after all you've done. Or perhaps you think, *If he really is God of the whole universe, why would he care about stumbling, tiny us?*

Maybe, like Roberta, you've suffered so much loss that you cannot believe in or bring yourself to try to talk to a God who says he loves you. Maybe you can't trust your own father, so why would you trust a heavenly Father? Or maybe you've tried the religious route, followed the rules, done everything right—and God feels further away than ever. And then what if you do pray, and pray fervently, and yet God doesn't seem to answer? Or the answer is the opposite of what you ask for?

We have so many good reasons to stay silent and distant from whoever God is. And, we think, he has even more reasons to dwell far from us.

But surely we want and hope for more? Yes, God is mysterious, invisible, and unfathomable, but most of us have also heard that God loves us and wants a relationship with us. How do we find this? How do we experience that love in a real and lasting way?

Let me invite you, dear fellow weary traveler, into these pages, into a new place that is not far or hard to get to. We can ditch our fears and our failures and come before God as we are right now—with all that we are and all that we are not. We're going to learn how to bring our whole selves before God, no matter what we're thinking and feeling, even when we have no words. And we're going to hear God speak back to us through his Word.

Don't worry. I'm not promising you ten simple steps to a foolproof prayer life or some kind of fake hack to intimacy with God. Instead, we're going to learn how our own stories and voices can lead us to a lasting attachment to the God who loves us. And to do this, we'll be embarking on a pathway to God that is ancient, yet we'll see and experience it anew.

We're not the first to struggle with prayer, with reaching out to this mysterious God. Listen to these cries:

Why, LORD, do you stand far off?[1]

Why do you hide your face?[2]

Why are you so far from helping me?[3]

How long, LORD?[4]

I get nothing but trouble all day long.[5]

Turn, O LORD, and deliver my soul.[6]

Have mercy on me, O God. . . . Wash me clean from my guilt.[7]

These words are, of course, from the Psalms. The psalmists felt distance, desperation, and doubt too. But they didn't remain there. So many times they landed somewhere else:

in a pasture, on the safety of a rock. They found the way to rest and trust:

The LORD is my shepherd.[8]

God is our refuge and strength.[9]

He set my feet on solid ground.[10]

Cast your burden on the LORD, and he will sustain you.[11]

This book of Scripture has been the prayer and song book of God's people for millennia. In my early years of faith, I knew bits and pieces of these 150 songs—mostly the well-known passages ("He makes me lie down in green pastures"[12]) and the choruses we sang in church each Sunday ("I Will Enter His Courts with Thanksgiving," "I Will Exalt Thee," "As a Deer Panteth for the Water"). I knew the Psalms were also Jesus' prayers and songs, that he quoted the Psalms more than any other book in the Old Testament. And I knew they were unique in the Bible for their poetic form and range of emotions and intimate window into the writers' innermost hearts—and these things both attracted and repelled me.

I came of age at a Christian college during a time when many in my faith context viewed emotions as suspect, as the saboteurs of right knowledge. The Christian life was about "knowing God," which meant endless Bible studies, word studies, contextual studies, sentence diagrams, biblical book outlines. Accurate theology was paramount. For someone like me, who truly wanted to know God, the course was clear: Get a minor in Greek and take as many Bible classes as possible. (I did both.) But the Psalms were poetry, which was hard to outline. And they were full of emotion. Though I had studied and composed poetry most of my life, prizing its beauty and economy of language, I dismissed these poem-prayers in God's Word as sentimental and theologically inconsequential. Give me Romans!

But as my life grew more complicated over the years, cracks and gaps began to show in my knowledge-only faith. By midlife, my husband and I had four kids, then were surprised by two more. I was teaching. We were commercial fishing in the Alaskan wilderness every summer. Our marriage was strained.

Then came the sixtieth straight day of being trapped in a house on a roadless island. The rain kept falling, the kids kept squabbling, and my husband and I had a fight. I couldn't sleep. I couldn't pray. All my knowledge and theology were little help. I needed more.

Exhausted, I turned to the Psalms on a whim, paging through one after another. And here, at the end of myself, when I felt like I couldn't even whisper my own words—I was riveted.

I cried out to God to hear me.[13]

By your words I can see where I'm going.[14]

I pray to you, O LORD, my rock.[15]

I will praise you, Lord my God, with all my heart.[16]

Give ear to my words, O LORD.[17]

That day, a realization hit me. Surely I "knew" it in the knowledge corner of my brain, but I suddenly felt the force of these words as never before. Within God's great story in Scripture—all the narratives of failure and victory, rebellion, intimacy with God—God draws near and speaks again and again. God thunders and weeps. God warns and woos. He speaks from fire and clouds, from mountains, through donkeys and children, and in the voices of men thought mad. Then Jesus arrives, and sometimes he speaks plainly, other times in riddles and stories. But always—God speaks.

Then—in the middle of all these words from God—here's a book of God's people speaking back. And what words these are! Not careful words, not words whispered fearfully to a far-distant God, not sedate or prim words of religious posturing—but words of anger, agony, despair, abandonment, anxiety; words of fierce hope, rejoicing, confidence.

I found myself stunned by an extraordinary reality: that the Holy Spirit inspired these writers to compose these yowls, doubts, and shouts; to sing these honest and unflinching, very human songs back to him. Yes, of course! Isn't this the heart of the whole enterprise of redemption: God's desire to be Immanuel, God-with-us? From the start in the garden taking long walks with his beloved friends, God revealed his heart to Eve and Adam and listened to theirs in response. What father does not wish to hear his children's hearts? God speaks to his people, his children, and the Psalms show us that he invites and even inspires us to speak back.

I had to try it myself. I found a quiet room, picked up a pen and a yellow legal pad, and, tremulously, began paging through the Psalms until I hit Psalm 13, a short psalm of lament by King David. It begins,

LORD, how long will You forget me?
Forever?
How long will You hide Your face from me?
How long will I store up anxious concerns within me,
agony in my mind every day?[18]

I couldn't believe how much David's words echoed my own emotions and experience. But reading silently on the page wasn't enough. In this moment of lack and longing, could these words be showing me the way?

I slowly wrote out David's verses in my journal. This simple step of slowing down and writing out each line of the psalm enabled me to hear it more clearly. But I found myself drawn deeper, needing to do more than repeat his words. I sensed an invitation to conversation. In between the verses, following his pattern, I began to write my own questions, my own circumstances, my own pleas to God.

I was tentative at first. I didn't want to twist the Psalms into an exercise of egocentric spirituality, nor did I want to remake God in my own image. But as I wrote, David's words from the midst of his life gave me language to break my silence, to bring my own circumstances and my own sagging heart into God's presence. I realized that this fuller engagement with the Psalms could help move God from my head into my present reality.

When I was done, I read my words aloud to my Father God. I was astounded. My words opened my ears wider to God's words. This was not a monologue, then; this was a holy dialogue with the living God. I felt it immediately: relief. The joy of reconnection. I understood in a deeper way that God was with me, and that he had spoken into my heart through his Word.

How I needed this! Over the course of my life, a knowledge-only approach has made it hard for me to attach myself to God with the connection and intimacy I long for. Yes, I revel in studying his attributes, in exploring points of doctrine and theology. Yet for most of my life I have struggled to believe he loves me. I have struggled to fully trust. Many of us do.

Researchers in the field of neurotheology[19] help us

understand why we experience such a profound gap between our knowledge of God and his Word and our ability to believe and actually live in and out of what we know. In *The Other Half of Church*, spiritual-formation pastor Michael Hendricks and neurotheologian Jim Wilder reveal that the left-brained, knowledge-only pursuit of spiritual growth—through Bible studies and sermons—engages the rational portion of our brains but ignores the right side, the relational half—which specializes in emotions, memories, and connectedness.[20] We usually ignore the body as well, creating a neck-up theology of prayer rather than bringing our integrated selves before God. Jessie Cruickshank, a minister and Harvard-trained expert in neuroscience and spiritual formation, urges us toward a holistic faith: "We must approach Scripture with our whole selves, whole stories, and whole bodies as a means by which we can encounter the author of all life, rather than as facts to retain or truth to know."[21]

I stumbled upon these insights and the unique power of the Psalms on my own. That day, while I was trapped on that roadless island, the Psalms began to teach me a profound lesson: We are not meant to stay distant, mere observers or passive listeners to stories and information about God. The Psalms invite us into holy conversation with a Father who longs to dwell as near to us as our next breath.

It's no accident that these prayer-songs are written in poetic form. Poetry accesses a part of us that arguments and

theological treatises cannot touch. Its verses, images, metaphors, rhythms, and wordplays move us through illumina-
tion rather than argument. When both sides of our brains
are lighting up—both the rational cells in one half, and the
images, feelings, and senses in the other—we experience
deeper engagement and real change.

If we long to connect with God, then, we need to pursue him with the whole brain—right side and left—as well
as with our bodies, which is another way that we are to
love the Lord our God with all our heart, soul, mind, and
strength.[22]

What does this kind of relationship with God look and
sound like? The Psalms show us. As we read them, they
usher us into intimate conversations between God and his
(ancient) people. But what if they are intended as more?
What if the psalmists' prayer-songs not only give us the
language for prayer but also model how to pray? What if
we can do more than repeat these expressions of lament
and praise? What if we can learn from them how to name
our own emotions and bring our own laments and praises
to God?

Six times in the Psalms the psalmists write exultantly
about singing a "new song"![23] This book of Scripture contains more than just one prayer of praise, or one song of
repentance, or a single cry of lament to God. David alone
penned more than seventy psalms, each in response to specific events in his life and the state of his heart. This man who
was after God's own heart[24] called out to his loving Father,

through the psalms, from the depths and heights of his days. Can we not do the same?

I've been writing and speaking to my Father, using the pathway of the Psalms, for almost twenty years now. I have written and prayed through a faith crisis; through difficult pregnancies; through a son's fury, a parent's death, another parent's rejection; through loneliness and hopelessness. I have not stopped, and I've led others into this powerful practice as well. I have seen this journey of prayer transform again and again—in my life, and in the lives of many others.

Here, in these pages, we'll explore seven different forms of the Psalms. In each one, we'll learn new but ancient ways to pray:

- lament
- wisdom
- trust
- confession
- creation
- thanksgiving
- praise

In each chapter, we'll learn about the fascinating approaches of these psalms, the movement and intentionality in their prayers. We'll learn how to listen closely to the verses and the psalmists' hearts. We'll follow Israel's story through the Psalms. And where the Psalms invite us in, we'll enter. At the end of each chapter, we'll **Draw Near**, learning a practice of writing and praying into these words. As we do, we'll find ourselves getting closer to the heart of God.

We won't just stay in our heads with this practice. Judy Mandeville, a dancer who has spent a lifetime practicing and teaching sacred movement, will help us rediscover what the ancient Hebrews knew about prayer, praise, and worship. They worshiped God holistically, using bodily postures and movements as well as their voices. Judy will offer movement suggestions and postures that will provide a fresh yet ancient way of encountering God, helping us bring not only our minds and emotions to prayer but our bodies as well.

As we pursue this practice of praying and writing into the Psalms, we follow those who have gone before us—those who have stumbled and fallen and despaired and danced and triumphed on the long path from far away to nearly and dearly beloved. God himself, who does not dwell far from us but is as close as our next breath, invites us on this journey. Will we follow?

■ draw near

In my time using and teaching the Psalms as a path into prayer, I've found seven powerful ways to enter, engage, and draw near to God. Here's a simple acronym that captures these activities:

NEARING

- **N**otate (Write out the original psalm by hand, an action that uses both sides of the brain.)
- **E**xpress (Use your voice and body gestures/movements to give full expression to the psalm.)
- **A**mplify (Add your response/circumstance/witness to the psalm.)
- **R**ead (Understand the original psalm in its context, reading different versions if desired.)
- **I**dentify (Personalize the psalm to you and/or to your faith community.)
- **N**ew Testament Fulfillment (Add relevant New Testament verses that augment and fulfill the message of the psalm.)
- **G**ather (Share psalm-prayers in worship with your faith community.)

In the **Draw Near** section of each chapter of this book, I'll lead us through one or more of these holistic activities with chosen psalms.

As we go through this process of praying through the Psalms, I want to be clear about what we're doing. We're not rewriting Scripture. We're not standing over God's Word as editors, tweaking and twisting as we choose. The Psalms cannot rewrite us if we are rewriting the Psalms. Instead, we are allowing the Psalms to teach us to pray, to guide our own words and emotions as we seek God's face, and to lead us to listen more closely to the response of his Word.

How will we do that? As we write into and out of the

Psalms, we'll keep in mind some hermeneutical guidelines to follow along the way:

- Before we write into a psalm, we'll seek to understand it first in its historical and theological context.

- We'll stay within the central subject and intent of the psalm.

- We will preserve the theology of the psalm: what it says about God's character, his nature, his acts in history, his attributes.

- We will write and speak into and out of the psalm to illustrate, witness, and respond to the truths of God's Word, not to alter them. We're not adding to the Word of God; we're allowing the Word of God to shape our own conversations with him.

To begin, you'll need a journal or some paper. If you have a journal that you write in regularly, you can use that, or you may start a new journal dedicated to this practice of communing with God.

After years of this practice, I now have a small stack of these journals. I open them often. I read and catch my breath each time: I am standing on holy ground—again. I see all the ways God met me through the Psalms in those moments and all the ways his responses brought freedom, joy, and closeness to him even in the darkest times. I am certain you will experience the same.

chapter one

entering through the open gate

Psalm 1

[1] Oh, the joys of those who do not
follow the advice of the wicked,
or stand around with sinners,
or join in with mockers.
[2] But they delight in the law of the LORD,
meditating on it day and night.
[3] They are like trees planted along the riverbank,
bearing fruit each season.
Their leaves never wither,
and they prosper in all they do.

[4] But not the wicked!
They are like worthless chaff, scattered by the wind.
[5] They will be condemned at the time of judgment.
Sinners will have no place among the godly.
[6] For the Lord watches over the path of the godly,
but the path of the wicked leads to destruction.

I have just turned thirteen. And now, because I've reached this magnificent age, I'm invited to a sledding party. A friend of my older sister's, a girl named Cheryl who lives in another town and goes to a church almost an hour away, has invited me. I have no idea what she means by youth group, but a party? That I understand. Parties are rare—and now I can go.

I don't know any of these other kids, and they're all older than me. I'm wearing the only cool pants I own: mustard-yellow-and-blue-pinstriped bell-bottoms. I try to have fun, but I'm deeply self-conscious.

When the ninth run down the long hill is not as fun as the second and third, we retreat. Our hands red with cold, we follow a young man that everyone calls pastor into a little white church. I sit next to Cheryl in a pew, and the man begins to talk. What is this? I've never heard of someone giving a talk at a party. But his face is kind, his voice gentle. He's telling us about Jesus. How Jesus came to take away our sins—all the ways we disobey God. I think of a lie I told last month. And my stealing. I've been stealing candy from the Peterson's Store and the A&P for a while now. I stole a pair of fingernail clippers from Mary's house last week. A pair of shorts from Kmart last month. I take things because I don't know how else to get them, but it weighs on me.

I listen to his words. *He came here for you. Jesus came for you and died for you. Because God wants you. God wants you to be his sons and daughters. He loves you, and he has a wonderful plan for your life.*

I cannot move. Every word hits me at my core. How does

this man know? I have been looking for this all my life. Yes, my short life—but it's been a long life for me so far.

That moment in that tiny country church was decades ago, but I remember it so clearly. I shot my hand up and walked down the aisle that day. I saw a path there, a path I had never known before. All my time in the beautiful woods around my house had shown me a force that loved the world, and I also knew I didn't know that force, whatever it was. But I wanted to.

I knew other things, though. I knew parents couldn't be trusted. I knew *I* couldn't be trusted. I knew that anger and hate were contagious and destructive and almost impossible to overcome. That the world was split into the lucky and the unlucky, and that nothing could breach that divide.

I had hoped a God was there. Many nights I tried to pray, but I felt my words bouncing off the walls of my room. But that day in the church, I finally believed he was real and close and . . . he wanted me? I prayed tremulously, and for the first time, I felt like God heard me.

I knew very little about the Bible then. I had not even heard of the Psalms. But I understood the choice before me: Go this way, or go the other way. Go toward God, or go away from God. Choose God, or choose yourself. And here's where those choices take you: God is with you every step, or you're separated from God and destruction awaits.

The Psalms and our journey of prayer begin here too.

One hundred fifty psalms were mostly composed over a six-hundred-year period, and as a general rule, no one knows what psalms were written when. But the editors who later compiled and ordered the psalms chose this prayer-song as the first. No wonder. Psalm 1 gestures forward to all the psalms that follow. It's a wisdom psalm, showing us the way to a wise and prosperous life.

This psalm is for all of us who feel an ache for the kind of flourishing life it describes. For we are a special kind of weary, are we not? We're now years into a culture hostile and divided, into toxic politics, the church shrinking and divided, disruption from the pandemic, war in Ukraine, so much sickness, death, and destruction. And we bear our own individual challenges, each of us. After thirty-four years of raising children, I saw my last son leave home. My house is empty. All my children live thousands of miles away. Our fishing business is threatened. Winter has wrapped its dark, icy fingers around our island in Alaska. A sense of isolation hangs over me like a shroud. And I struggle to break free from the ache of estrangement from a parent. Some days I feel like an exile. Some days I have neither words nor even a desire to pray.

Do you feel this weariness too? Psalm 1 reminds us of what we ache for, leading us all the way back to Genesis, to that perfect, paradisaical garden when the world was new and man's and woman's hearts and path were undivided. They ate from the trees in the garden and walked and conversed face-to-face with their loving Creator.

But we know what happened. They turned away, stopped trusting their Father. They listened to the wrong voice, choosing to believe the serpent's words rather than their Father's.

They went their own way, on the path that led outside the garden. The path to separation and death. They became exiles. Psalm 1 shows us this path too. The gate before us invites us into this grand book of green pastures, of God's sheltering wings, of stars shouting God's glory, trees clapping their hands, and so many cries and rescues from the pit and the miry clay. But before us we also see another choice: the path that leads in the opposite direction, to futility and finally ruin.

This same choice is offered to God's people in the book of Joshua. Moses has just died. Joshua is about to lead the whole motley crew of a vast multitude of Hebrews into the land God promised generations earlier. But before they set a single foot into the land, God speaks these words:

> Be strong and very courageous. Be careful to obey all the law my servant Moses gave you; do not turn from it to the right or to the left, that you may be successful wherever you go. Keep this Book of the Law always on your lips; meditate on it day and night, so that you may be careful to do everything written in it. Then you will be prosperous and successful.[1]

Do you hear how these words are echoed in Psalm 1? Gordon J. Wenham, author of *Psalms as Torah*, writes,

> From the very first psalm, the Psalter presents itself as a second Torah, divided into five books like the Pentateuch, and it invites its readers to meditate

on them day and night, just as Joshua was told to meditate on the law of Moses.[2]

These words, this invitation to choose the path to life, were not just for ancient Israel. Are we not Eve and Adam as well? Are we not wanderers in the wilderness? Don't we all keep choosing to walk our own way?

But here we stand at the gate, our exiled hearts longing for God—and look! We're invited back. We can return to the garden God fashioned for us. We can so delight in God's words and presence that we're dripping with fruit, our leaves green through every season, prosperity blossoming around us.

But we've got to take the first step inside. If we want to draw nearer to this God who invites, we can't simply gaze through the gate. We've got to bring our whole selves through the gate—our bodies, minds, hearts, souls, spirits. We do want to grow in knowledge, but we have to do more than "know God." We're here to *meet* God. If we are to find him, to draw nearer to this God who says he is here with us, then let us try to meet him on his terms rather than ours.

I know no better way to do this than through the words of Scripture. I've come to believe that God's Word is what it says it is: authoritative, holy, and inspired by God himself. That means these words are alive. I've studied language and literature for most of my life, but I've discovered nothing that moves, inspires, pierces, empowers, shakes, and shapes as God's Word does.

But maybe you have doubts. Maybe you've not read the

Bible much. Maybe you don't trust the Bible much. Maybe you feel like an outsider to all this. That's okay. I felt like that for a long time as well. It's okay to begin with questions instead of answers. I've led people into the Psalms who were unsure about the Bible, yet they shared the ache, the longing, the search for the good path; they decided to experiment and experience it for themselves. That's a good start. Who knows where it can lead?

The Psalms themselves give us this stunning image of who we can be: "I run in the path of your commandments, for you have set my heart free."[3] This path of relearning prayer is a journey into deeper love, into deeper attachment to God. And we're not walking, we're running! We're running free and fast because we're running on the path that leads to the God who made us, who loves us, who longs for us to come near.

Are we ready to take that first step? Let's begin!

■ draw near

The open gate is our first invitation to explore this new yet old pathway to prayer. If you are struggling with doubt or uncertainty as you begin, let me encourage you with this perspective from Heidi, a fellow God-seeker who has written into and out of the Psalms with me:

> What could I add to these ancient words? My
> experiences today? I feel strangely common, just a
> tiny voice in the cacophony of millions who cried
> the same human tears, sang the same sad songs. I feel

like a raindrop in a torrential rain. A snowflake in an avalanche. A single note in a symphony. How can my words matter? But then, as I continue to read and write, I hear the Voice between the lines, the Voice who chose the writers, those heralds, called to weave humanity and God together. I can feel the Heart of the One who says, "Pay attention! This is for you!" I hear an almighty, all-knowing call: "I SEE YOU. I KNOW YOU. I LOVE YOU."[4]

Remember, our simple acronym will guide our psalm-prayers:

NEARING

- **N**otate (Write out the original psalm by hand, an action that uses both sides of the brain.)
- **E**xpress (Use your voice and body gestures/movements to give full expression to the psalm.)
- **A**mplify (Add your response/circumstance/witness to the psalm.)
- **R**ead (Understand the original psalm in its context, reading different versions if desired.)
- **I**dentify (Personalize the psalm to you and/or to your faith community.)
- **N**ew Testament Fulfillment (Add relevant New Testament verses that augment and fulfill the message of the psalm.)
- **G**ather (Share psalm-prayers in worship with your faith community.)

As we take our first steps and **Draw Near** in psalm-praying, writing into and out of the Psalms, let's keep in mind our hermeneutical guidelines:

- Before we write into a psalm, we'll seek to understand it first in its historical and theological context.

- We'll stay within the central subject and intent of the psalm.

- We will preserve the theology of the psalm: what it says about God's character, his nature, his acts in history, his attributes.

- We will write and speak into and out of the Psalms to illustrate, witness, and respond to the truths of God's Word, not to alter them. We're not adding to the Word of God; we're allowing the Word of God to shape our own conversations with him.

Pull out your chosen journal or paper.

In this first psalm and in this first chapter, we'll start with four simple but powerful exercises:

1. **Read** and understand the original psalm in its context, in different versions if desired.

2. **Notate** the psalm (write it out by hand).

3. **Identify** with the psalm (personalize the psalm to you).

4. **Express** the psalm. You may wish to do this silently. However, reading aloud also engages the larynx, diaphragm, and ears; the more of ourselves we employ, the greater our attention to our psalm-prayer.

Read

It might seem obvious, but this first step is crucial. God inspired these words within the Israelites' own story and particular historical context. Paradoxically and wonderfully, the more we sit with and grasp the original story, the more we're able to engage with the psalm and apply it to our own story. To help with this process, I like to read several different translations.

I'm including two of my favorites here for you to consider. Because I don't know Hebrew, I like to start with a literal translation, to get as close as possible to the original language, before moving on to a more contemporary translation.

Psalm 1 (YOUNG'S LITERAL TRANSLATION)

¹ O the happiness of that one, who
　　Hath not walked in the counsel of the wicked.
　　And in the way of sinners hath not stood,
　　And in the seat of scorners hath not sat;
² But—in the law of Jehovah [is] his delight,
　　And in His law he doth meditate by day and by night:
³ And he hath been as a tree,
　　Planted by rivulets of water,
　　That giveth its fruit in its season,

And its leaf doth not wither,
    And all that he doth he causeth to prosper.
[4] Not so the wicked:
    But—as chaff that wind driveth away!
[5] Therefore the wicked rise not in judgment,
    Nor sinners in the company of the righteous,
[6] For Jehovah is knowing the way of the righteous,
    And the way of the wicked is lost!

Psalm 1 (NLT)

[1] Oh, the joys of those who do not
    follow the advice of the wicked,
    or stand around with sinners,
    or join in with mockers.
[2] But they delight in the law of the LORD,
    meditating on it day and night.
[3] They are like trees planted along the riverbank,
    bearing fruit each season.
Their leaves never wither,
    and they prosper in all they do.

[4] But not the wicked!
    They are like worthless chaff, scattered by the wind.
[5] They will be condemned at the time of judgment.
    Sinners will have no place among the godly.
[6] For the LORD watches over the path of the godly,
    but the path of the wicked leads to destruction.

Notate

Our next step is choosing a version (either from the ones given here or another translation you prefer) and then handwriting the psalm. Taking pen in hand helps us slow down to soak in the Word of God. Our eyes translate the words into impulses that move our hands deliberately across the journal paper. Our body is giving shape to God's words. We're listening to God, understanding the sense and movement of the psalm from beginning to end.

In this practice of notating, we're already "meditating" on his law. The root of the Hebrew word translated *meditate* means "to murmur," suggesting intense and outwardly expressed concentration. As we write the psalm by hand, we must ponder each word in much the same way as if we were speaking it aloud. Neuroscience tells us that writing by hand calls on both sides of the brain: the language mode of the left brain and the visuospatial and nonverbal, memory-rich modes of the right brain. Also, writing by hand (as opposed to writing on a keyboard) increases understanding and recall.[5] In this simple exercise of writing God's Word by hand, we are integrating body, mind, memory, and spirit.

1. As you **Notate** the verses, leave two or three lines of space between each verse to make room for the next activity.

2. Be intentional with your handwriting (print, cursive, calligraphy, etc.), considering what style feels fitting to the psalm.

3. Carefully consider the meaning of each verse as you write.

Identify

These words of wisdom and admonition are written for all people, which means each of us as well. When we step into the verses personally, using the first-person *I*, the psalm comes closer, drawing us into the "story" and nearer to God's heart. As we engage Psalm 1, we will also discover that God is not inviting us simply to consider two paths of life—he's asking us which path we will choose.

In the space you left beneath each line of the psalm, write the verses again, this time identifying yourself directly as the audience.

Leslie's Psalm 1 prayer

Oh, the joys of those who do not
    follow the advice of the wicked,
    or stand around with sinners,
    or join in with mockers.

Oh, the joys I, Leslie, will know when I don't
    follow the advice of the wicked,
    or stand around with sinners;
    when I don't join in with mockers.

Express

Your final step, when you've finished notating, is to **Express** your psalm-prayer. This could be a silent exercise, but reading aloud engages the body and senses. Consider as well adding a gesture or a posture that expresses your words. The more of ourselves we employ, the greater our attention to our psalm-prayer as we enact it before our Father. Here are some possible movements:

- Verses 1-2: Head up, arms down and palms open to the side

- Verses 2-3: Lifting arms slowly overhead (pausing to feel the expanse of the tree imagery)

- Verses 4-6: Head down and hands crossed sharply over your face

Or create your own physical expression as you read your psalm-prayer to God. He is listening!

crying out in lament

Psalm 2:1-3 (NLT)

¹Why are the nations so angry?
Why do they waste their time with
futile plans?
²The kings of the earth prepare for battle;
the rulers plot together
against the LORD
and against his anointed one.
³"Let us break their chains," they cry,
"and free ourselves from slavery
to God."

Psalm 3:1-2 (NIV)

A PSALM OF DAVID. WHEN HE FLED FROM HIS SON ABSALOM.

¹LORD, how many are my foes!
How many rise up against me!
²Many are saying of me,
"God will not deliver him."

We are on the way home now, the youth pastor at the wheel. I'm wet and cold from the sledding party. But I don't want to go home, don't want to break this spell.

"Do you have a church to go to?" the pastor asks, glancing at me as he navigates the winding, icy dirt road. I think briefly of the Congregational church, the only church in our little town.

"No," I say. "There's only one church in town, and we can't get to it."

"That's okay," he tells me. "You have God's Word right there in your hands." I am holding a small brown Bible that he has given me.

"Spend some time every day reading it and praying. That's how you can grow in your faith. God's not going to leave you, Leslie," he says kindly. I tear up.

We pull into the driveway to my house, a white Cape Cod that is more than 150 years old. I am carrying the biggest secret in the world inside me. I know my prayer was heard, maybe for the first time ever. I raised my hand, I chose a new path. I'm holding a little book filled with words, words from God himself. I don't know much about these words, but I know I am different. How will I live now in this house with this secret?

I cannot tell my mother. I cannot tell my father, who drifts in and out of our lives like a heavy ghost.

My father drives off every day as a traveling salesman, but sales are few. He is fired from one job and then another and another until he is no longer hired at all. I understand why, even as a child. I see that he cannot look anyone in the face. That he doesn't seem to see us or anyone else. That he glides along in a separate world. That he doesn't express feelings or sadness or any kind of emotion that I can recognize. I know as a twelve-year-old that he will never—that he cannot—change. There is nothing to him but flesh and silence, yet his presence evokes rage. Whenever he shows up, we all try to disappear.

Every day the family news is broadcast across the house: The bank will repossess the house, the electricity will be turned off, there's no money left. We're eating boiled soybeans for dinner twice a week, canned mackerel two other nights. The house quakes with thrown plants, crashing dishes, screams and shouts. I plug my ears, shaking.

My secret feels small and impotent now, distant. What good does it do to open that little brown book? God cannot live here. I leave it in my drawer.

At the end of my freshman year, we move again. To another town, another school. We live in a two-hundred-year-old house surrounded by fields and deciduous woods. In the summer we find berries, and our well goes dry, and we haul buckets of creek water across those wide, beautiful fields. In the winter, with no insulation and only a single woodstove for heat, we freeze. We tear the house apart to restore it, living in sawdust and chaos for years. No one is allowed in.

I walk the last mile home one day, dropped off by a neighbor. I am sixteen now. I step through the screen door and into the kitchen, wary. I don't know who is home and what might be happening.

This day a cyclone has hit again. A few old upholstered chairs and some wooden hard-backed chairs are strewn around the room, turned over. A table lies on its side. Above, on the yellow-plastered walls, someone has written a dirty name. Not on one wall but on three walls, the red paint still dripping. My stomach clenches. I suck in my breath. I'm grateful to have missed this particular show, but maybe it's not over. I drop my books, leave the house, and run into the woods. The woods are quiet and safe.

My second week at the new school, a girl in one of my classes invites me to a Bible study. A Bible study? What is that? But my heart leaps, my conscience turns, and I dig out the little brown book given to me two years before.

On my first visit, we are reading in a book called John. Suddenly I am starving, I am thirsty, because I am hearing— again, or is it the first time?—words about Jesus that awaken everything in me that's dead. And it is not long before I am reaching for my Bible every night, my hands like roots, plunging deep into pages and passages. I go to this Bible study every week. I am memorizing verses. I am praying. I am the only one carrying my Bible on top of my books every day at school. I am the holy roller, the Jesus girl, the weird one. And I don't care. I am glimpsing a reality so much bigger than the tiny world I live in. I am glimpsing love.

At home, three of us ask to go to church on Sunday

mornings. We already know the answer: no. We have to work. Every weekend and some weeknights we are haying for the goats, roofing the barn, cutting down trees, chopping wood for that one woodstove in the great room to keep the temperature there, in that room alone, above freezing. There is no time for church, we are told.

Inside our cold house, I do not speak of these things to my siblings, nor they to me. We have no language to voice our loneliness and suffering. No one wants to hear it; no one can change it.

I didn't know then about the lament psalms, psalms that voice with startling honesty the writers' anguish and anxieties. I needed those words and those prayers. And I would not have been shocked at how soon they appear in the book of prayers.

In the beginning of this prayer book, we find two ways of life: one that ends in nothingness, the other in happiness. But what do our first steps look like along the good path? Psalm 2, the very next prayer-song, takes us to an entirely different place:

Why do the nations conspire
    and the peoples plot in vain?
The kings of the earth rise up
    and the rulers band together
    against the LORD and against his anointed, saying,
"Let us break their chains
    and throw off their shackles."[1]

With a turn of the page we've left the riverbank, the tree brimming with fruit. We see before us the nations, kings and rulers clustering, fomenting rebellion with fists raised against God, defiant.

What is this? If I were the editor of this collection, I would want the songbook of God's people to revel in a little more blessedness, a little more beauty: another tree, another river, birds, visions heavenly and otherworldly for those who are obedient to God's Word and God's ways. I would expect songs of praise. After all, the Hebrew name for the book of Psalms is *Tehillim*, meaning "praises." And yes, there are many songs of praise in this book of praises—but not for a while. First, next, and again and again, the psalmists lament. Lament is an expression of sorrow, grief, complaint. Fully a third of the 150 psalms are lament psalms, and here, in this first book out of five books in the Second Torah, lament dominates.

But isn't this second psalm telling the truth? I love God and want to follow him, and then I must return home and open the door to my house. This is the world I began to glimpse, even then as a teenager, and this is the world we know now, some three thousand years after the writing of this psalm: a world fractured, separated from God, angry, defiant. While we may choose the right path, many of those in power will choose the other, and all of us under their power will suffer. How hopeful and happy is this?

Perhaps the next psalm will return us to the peaceful path. Psalm 3 is David's song. He's writing as king. He's the king who loves God more than any king before or after him. Surely now, with the unlimited power of God and the authority of the throne, all will be well. Now we'll return to halcyon orchards and ever-fruited trees! But David has something else to say:

> LORD, how many are my foes!
> How many rise up against me!
> Many are saying of me,
> "God will not deliver him."[2]

We are only to the third prayer, and here is David, the king, running from his own son. We're plunged into the despairing heart of a father whose son wants to murder him. Surely this psalm is an anomaly, and those that follow will be different. But no. Here is how the next three psalms begin:

> Answer me when I call to you,
> my righteous God.
> Give me relief from my distress;
> have mercy on me and
> hear my prayer.[3]

> Listen to my words, LORD,
> consider my lament.
> Hear my cry for help,
> my King and my God,
> for to you I pray.[4]

> Have mercy on me, LORD, for I am faint;
> heal me, LORD, for my bones are in agony.
> My soul is in deep anguish.
> How long, LORD, how long?[5]

By now, six psalms in, we are surely wondering: *Were we wrong to trust in God?* We enter the gate of faith, we open the prayer book for God's people, we are changed—but the world is not. The world is as fractured and as bent against God and his people as ever. And surely the fractures feel greater now because our eyes and souls are fully awake. We begin to realize we might always be strangers in this cracked, crooked land. And if that is so, we will surely need words of lament.

Thank God, that is what we're given. In God's prayer book, there will be no dress-up or fakery along this path to prayer, no vapid, pious words. The editors of the Psalms, who arranged these prayers and songs as a commentary and guide for God's people to live wisely and well in their sojourn, knew to take us here next, to the truth of this life. So yes, even as we choose the God path instead of the no-God path, we often find ourselves in a tangle of brambles. Yes, Yahweh is in charge, the King over all kings. And in the second psalm we're already given the promise that a Messiah is coming. We're given that lifeline. And if I root myself in his Word and his law, I will be blessed and happy, but look: How many are my foes! My soul is in deep anguish! How long, Lord, how long? Have mercy on me and hear my prayer! Answer me when I call to you!

King David wrote all these words because they're the truth of his story, the truth of his heart.

Do you know his story? David is the youngest of eight sons, just a teenage shepherd boy whom no one would notice. But he is chosen to be the next king of Israel. No one can believe it, likely not even David himself. But David says yes, he chooses back, because among all his brothers, he is the one who loves God completely. Then what comes next? A short waltz to the throne, the smooth assumption of power, the blessed, happy life of one who walks the God path?

No. It's fifteen years before David is crowned. Fifteen years of living as a fugitive, fleeing and hiding from King Saul, who wants to kill him and keep the throne. What did that feel and sound like for David? We know exactly: He wrote some of these lament psalms during those years.

Who does not understand this? Who does not know the pain of divine silence, the palpable yearning for an invisible God to appear and shake the quaking world to rights? The Israelites who later sang David's songs in worship at the Temple certainly did. Their story from the start is a tale of woes and foes, generations of slavery in Egypt. This was a people constantly under siege from nations bent on obliterating them. And even in times of relative peace and security, the Israelites would need these laments again and again.

And we do as well, every one of us. Because if we are honest, and especially if we are living and rooting ourselves in God's words and God's story, we need this kind of vocabulary. The more we love righteousness, the more we feel distress when wrong prevails and wickedness rules.

And we must be honest about ourselves as well. We do not always long for the right. We are weak, we are selfish, we are prideful, we make mistakes, we bring misery to ourselves and others through our sin. We stumble and fall—and so we cry out.

We are not alone in our laments. God himself laments. Yahweh, the sovereign Creator, all-powerful and perfect in holiness, lacking nothing—this God cries out in lament over his people who have rebelled and rejected his love again and again. God on his throne does not bear this pain impassively. No, he wails:

> How can I give you up, O Ephraim?
> How can I hand you over, O Israel?
> How can I make you like Admah?
> How can I treat you like Zeboiim?
> My heart recoils within me;
> my compassion grows warm and tender.[6]

Do you hear it? God himself knows the anguish of rejection and betrayal, and he speaks it again and again throughout the stories of his people.

Jesus, too, laments. Not long before he is crucified, he looks down over Jerusalem, into her city streets and back through time, seeing all the prophets sent to call God's people back to his great love—and the stubborn hearts of the people who would not listen:

O Jerusalem, Jerusalem, the city that kills the prophets and stones God's messengers! How often I have wanted to gather your children together as a hen protects her chicks beneath her wings, but you wouldn't let me. And now, look, your house is abandoned and desolate.[7]

And in his final hours, hanging from the cross, Jesus utters David's own words, the most chilling lament of all: "My God, my God, why have you forsaken me?"[8]

Can we dare such language too? Can sons and daughters truly speak to their Father like this? And yes, we are sons and daughters, but we are also the dust of the earth, fitted with clay feet and a tiny earthen tongue. How can we presume to wag our human complaints at the Sovereign One on heaven's throne? How can we, the pottery, say to the potter, "How could you?" What kind of God would allow such audacity?

The God who made woman and man to walk with him face-to-face in the garden in the cool of the evening. Who rescued Noah and his family, not giving up on humankind, though all others had turned to violence. Who entered into an eternal covenant relationship with Abraham, a mere human, his own creation, and then extended that covenant to all who would come after and set their hope and trust and love upon him. The God who came to earth as a mewling newborn in a feeding trough to save his people and who chose ordinary men and women to walk and eat and spend every single day with him.

He keeps choosing us, we who are so small and limited and weak. He wants us. He died to make us his.

Such love is almost too much to believe. But now that it is ours, we know, even instinctively, that this love must include honest, soul-deep conversation. How can God ask us to love him with all we have and all we are if we cannot speak the fullness of our hearts to him, whether in love or in pain? Prayer, then, must be a dialogue, a chance to speak freely and be heard, even when the words are jagged and hard.

But lament is ultimately hopeful. Lament grieves over the way things are right now, and yet it dares to believe that our Father can and will do something about it. Lament builds a verbal bridge between our broken reality and the reality of a Father who listens and responds.

Even as I write this, I marvel. I think of parents who have little interest in the thoughts and even the heartbreaks of their children. I think of a lifetime of covering and pretending and denying and remaining silent around the things closest to my own heart so as not to provoke anger and rejection within my own family. How beyond comprehension it is, then, that the holy God who sees all has opened his ears to our ugliest guttural cries and hurts! He accepts our accusations. He wants us to wail to him!

And in that moment of complaint, fear, and rock-bottom desperation, something happens even while we are speaking. Even as the words emerge from our mouths, we are rescued from the corrosion and captivity of silence. "When I kept silent, my bones wasted away,"[9] David wrote—and is this not our story as well? Our cries join David's and the voices of thousands, millions of others, bereft, confused, alone, calling out for a Savior. And even in the first breaking of the silence, we find relief.

Because we could choose otherwise. Many of us have tried. We could be like the nations who defy God or the woman or man who chooses the second path away from God. In time of pain, we could give up on God, deny his presence. We could try distractions and addictions, from cannabis to Netflix. We could run to money, to success. We have lots of options, and we have tried so many of them. But here is something better.

We're each given a tongue, emotions, and an invitation from God to call to him when our hearts are shredded. "Where are you, God?" we cry, and even as we charge God with absence, we are inviting God into our pain. "How long, Lord, how long?" And in the very words we speak, we know we are no longer alone. We're in need of a God-rescue, and our lament opens our ears to his response. Lament opens our eyes to watch for what God will do.

This sounds like enough—the relief of speaking our pain,

the belief that God will join us in it. But there's more that happens within lament. In these psalms, these early laments of David, I have given only the beginning. I am not telling the whole story. Because yes, first the lament cries must be attended to. But so much more happens after these cries. A few stanzas later, the prayers end in a different place, in a changed voice:

Victory comes from you, O LORD.
May you bless your people.[10]

In peace I will lie down and sleep,
for you alone, O LORD, will keep me safe.[11]

But let all who take refuge in you rejoice;
let them sing joyful praises forever.
Spread your protection over them,
that all who love your name may be filled with joy.
For you bless the godly, O LORD;
you surround them with your shield of love.[12]

The LORD has heard my cry for mercy;
the LORD accepts my prayer.[13]

The broken-down reality that calls forth our deepest laments is not the only reality. How does the psalmist land here, in these places of calm and surety and even sleep, while surrounded by enemies? How do we account for this radical shift of heart and language?

Perhaps he waited, putting down his pen until the enemy soldiers ran off, defeated. Perhaps he turned from his cries until his opponents stopped their treasonous tongues, until Saul the king gave up on pursuing him, laid down his spear. Maybe David waited months, years even, to pen his halcyon endings.

If there were no listening, rescuing God in heaven above who desires to hear from his children, this explanation would make sense. But this is not the reality I know.

When we bring our pain to God, reality shifts. Our brains shift. When we write into and out of lament and then speak our prayer before God, we discover that while the crisis—the catalyzing event behind our lament—remains, it is smaller. Our present story of piercing and pain is now set into the grandest story of all: God is on his throne. Yahweh reigns! And he is here with us in our memories and our hardest stories to redeem them.

The minutes, even hours we spend writing into and out of the lament psalms will not immediately fix our situation, but they will enable us to "fix our eyes on Jesus, faith's pioneer and perfecter."[14] Lament can begin a new pattern of bringing the whole of ourselves and our experiences to God. When we do this, we are literally rewiring our brains and hearts.

Neuroscience has discovered that humans avoid memories

that are painful or traumatic, that our brains actually rewire in self-protection. The trauma is then stuck and hidden in our very cells, though the unhealed pain often bleeds into our thoughts and behaviors in other ways.[15] But when we instead reenter those places with language, when we invite our Father God into them, we can experience his loving presence even in the hardest of memories. We can move toward being freed from the tyranny of vivid pain. We can be freed to trust, to believe that nothing "will be able to separate us from the love of God."[16]

But I am not here to merely convince you of something I have experienced or others have known. I'm not here to impart theology and knowledge about the power of God. I'm not here to keep you safely distant, studying and cataloging God's redemptive acts. I am here to help you enter into God's story yourself, to experience God's right-now, rescuing power and presence. God is alive and active and ready for you to encounter him afresh, whole-brained, in his living Word. Bring him your pain. He is waiting.

■ draw near

Many of the lament psalms describe enemies and fierce opponents. Not many of us experience enemies out on a battlefield or people literally trying to take our lives, but we all experience spiritual battles. Sometimes the enemy is us—our own thoughts, habits, memories, sins. Sometimes we fight against aspects of the prevailing culture that run counter to

God's righteous laws. And we know we do have an enemy, Satan, who desires to destroy us:

> Finally, be strong in the Lord and in his mighty power. Put on the full armor of God, so that you can take your stand against the devil's schemes. For our struggle is not against flesh and blood, but against the rulers, against the authorities, against the powers of this dark world and against the spiritual forces of evil in the heavenly realms.[17]

Perhaps we wonder, though, what to do with laments that go a step further, into requests for God to destroy or harm the writer's physical enemies. These are called imprecatory psalms. How do we understand these words? Didn't Jesus tell us to love our enemies?[18]

We may begin to understand as we watch images of war's destruction, seeing innocents slaughtered. Sometimes nations and individuals unleash such harm that we're moved to pray for an end to the carnage and the evil. God's Word clearly allows for this.

Our motivation is key. In this kind of lament, we set aside any desire for personal revenge; rather, we lift the ache of injustice to our Father, to his righteous judgment. Most of the imprecatory psalms end in a place of peace, knowing Yahweh reigns, evil will be destroyed, and justice will prevail—in God's time. When we pray, God may also bring to mind ways we can righteously address and ameliorate the wrongdoing.

As you enter this practice of writing into the lament

psalms, identify the source of opposition as clearly as you can (my anger, my memories, the enemy, etc.). Release your desire to avenge, and hand it over to God, who is the only perfect judge. This step of calling out to God honestly and fully may be the most important step you take in your relationship with God. Here's what happened for Jenn, a participant in one of my classes, as she immersed herself in the Psalms this way:

> When I marinate in the Psalms, my crusty exoskeleton dissolves, exposing the tender areas I have tried to protect by my own means. The sacrifice God wants from me is to stop protecting my own heart, but instead to put my broken, bleeding heart into his hands, to trust him to hold it together, to protect it and to heal it. Coming from a past where emotion, tears, feelings were not validated but looked down upon (both in the church group as well as my family), Psalm 51:17 has been a tremendous comfort. God does not despise or look down on me if/when I cry. He comes near as I write into these psalms. And if I will let him, he holds my broken heart ever so gently.[19]

As we move into our practice, let's remember our acronym for entering into prayer through the Psalms:

NEARING

- **N**otate (Write out the original psalm by hand, an action that uses both sides of the brain.)
- **E**xpress (Use your voice and body gestures/movements to give full expression to the psalm.)
- **A**mplify (Add your response/circumstance/witness to the psalm.)
- **R**ead (Understand the original psalm in its context, reading different versions if desired.)
- **I**dentify (Personalize the psalm to you and/or to your faith community.)
- **N**ew Testament Fulfillment (Add relevant New Testament verses that augment and fulfill the message of the psalm.)
- **G**ather (Share psalm-prayers in worship with your faith community.)

In this exercise, we will **Read**, **Notate**, **Amplify**, and **Express** to engage with lament.

Read

Read through the lament psalms provided here (Psalm 6, Psalm 13, and Psalm 42), or look through the list of individual and communal psalms that follows. Choose the psalm that speaks to you the clearest right now in whatever challenging circumstances you're facing: an illness, the loss of a family member or friend, financial needs, difficult headlines, rejection by a friend or family member.

Psalm 6 (NLT)

FOR THE CHOIR DIRECTOR: A PSALM OF DAVID, TO BE ACCOMPANIED BY AN
EIGHT-STRINGED INSTRUMENT

¹ O Lord, don't rebuke me in your anger
    or discipline me in your rage.
² Have compassion on me, Lord, for I am weak.
    Heal me, Lord, for my bones are in agony.
³ I am sick at heart.
    How long, O Lord, until you restore me?

⁴ Return, O Lord, and rescue me.
    Save me because of your unfailing love.
⁵ For the dead do not remember you.
    Who can praise you from the grave?

⁶ I am worn out from sobbing.
    All night I flood my bed with weeping,
    drenching it with my tears.
⁷ My vision is blurred by grief;
    my eyes are worn out because of all
      my enemies.

⁸ Go away, all you who do evil,
    for the Lord has heard my weeping.
⁹ The Lord has heard my plea;
    the Lord will answer my prayer.
¹⁰ May all my enemies be disgraced and terrified.
    May they suddenly turn back in shame.

Psalm 13 (NLT)

FOR THE CHOIR DIRECTOR: A PSALM OF DAVID.

¹ O LORD, how long will you forget me? Forever?
How long will you look the other way?
² How long must I struggle with anguish
in my soul,
with sorrow in my heart every day?
How long will my enemy have the
upper hand?

³ Turn and answer me, O LORD my God!
Restore the sparkle to my eyes, or I will die.
⁴ Don't let my enemies gloat, saying, "We have
defeated him!"
Don't let them rejoice at my downfall.

⁵ But I trust in your unfailing love.
I will rejoice because you have rescued me.
⁶ I will sing to the LORD
because he is good to me.

Psalm 42 (NIV)

FOR THE DIRECTOR OF MUSIC. A *MASKIL* OF THE SONS OF KORAH.

¹ As the deer pants for streams of water,
so my soul pants for you, my God.
² My soul thirsts for God, for the living God.
When can I go and meet with God?
³ My tears have been my food
day and night,

while people say to me all day long,
  "Where is your God?"
⁴ These things I remember
  as I pour out my soul:
how I used to go to the house of God
  under the protection of the Mighty One
with shouts of joy and praise
  among the festive throng.

⁵ Why, my soul, are you downcast?
  Why so disturbed within me?
Put your hope in God,
  for I will yet praise him,
  my Savior and my God.

⁶ My soul is downcast within me;
  therefore I will remember you
from the land of the Jordan,
  the heights of Hermon—from Mount Mizar.
⁷ Deep calls to deep
  in the roar of your waterfalls;
all your waves and breakers
  have swept over me.

⁸ By day the LORD directs his love,
  at night his song is with me—
  a prayer to the God of my life.

⁹I say to God my Rock,
  "Why have you forgotten me?
Why must I go about mourning,
  oppressed by the enemy?"
¹⁰My bones suffer mortal agony
  as my foes taunt me,
saying to me all day long,
  "Where is your God?"

¹¹Why, my soul, are you downcast?
  Why so disturbed within me?
Put your hope in God,
  for I will yet praise him,
my Savior and my God.

Lament Psalms[20]

Individual

Psalms 2–7, 13, 17, 22, 25, 26, 28, 31, 35, 38, 39, 42, 43, 54–57, 59, 61, 63, 64, 69–71, 86, 88, 102, 109, 120, 130, 140–143

Communal

Psalms 44, 60, 74, 79, 80, 83, 106, 125

Notate

Write the psalm out by hand, one verse at a time. Through the physical act of writing, we're interiorizing God's words. Leave space below each verse for your amplification.

Amplify

In the practice of **Amplification**, we're adding our stories, our circumstances, our particular laments to our chosen psalm. Beneath each verse, respond in writing to the psalmist's words with your own emotions and circumstances. You can do this in journal form or follow the pattern of the Psalms and use a tighter poetic form. Take your time. This part can be done in one sitting or in several sittings.

Express

When you have finished amplifying, **Express** your psalm-prayer by bringing your body, your breath, your voice to these words. Sing the words you have written, pray them, read them loudly or softly. Let your body move into whatever posture rises organically from these words. Or consider these suggestions:

- A movement for reverence: *barak*, a Hebrew word meaning "to kneel," but also "to bless"
- A movement for lament: arms crossed over the stomach while bending and rocking at the waist
- A movement for anger: shaking clenched fists

To help illustrate this process of writing into lament, I've included brief excerpts of two people's psalm-prayers, each written in different circumstances. I encourage you to use these, not as direct influences on your own response, but as inspiration for how this kind of prayer can give voice to specific pain.

Sharon's Psalm 6 (NLT)

A LAMENT ON DEALING WITH A DIFFICULT MOTHER

O LORD, don't rebuke me in your anger
   or discipline me in your rage.

I know you have the right to be angry with me.
   I have failed so many times with my mother.
   Why do I always answer her back? Why do I take
      her bait?
   It seems I can never do or say anything right.

Have compassion on me, LORD, for I am weak.
   Heal me, LORD, for my bones are in agony.

I really need your mercy, Lord. I feel beaten up,
      weak.
   I'm not eating or sleeping. My bones and
      everything in my body are in pain.

I am sick at heart.
   How long, O LORD, until you restore me?

I am sick at heart indeed and tired of needing,
tired of grieving. How much longer, Lord?
You will restore me, I'm believing,
but how much longer, Lord?

Leslie's Psalm 13 (ESV)

A LAMENT ON A DIFFICULT SITUATION AT A FORMER CHURCH

How long, O LORD? Will you forget me forever?
How long will you hide your face from me?

Lord, you alone know how long, how deeply I've felt
trapped in this place alone; I've tried to make
the best of it for so long, shielding myself from
enemy taunts and threats, keeping my chin up,
resigned;
but I'm getting desperate. Add to it the pressure upon my
livelihood, it's too much! Anxiety is pulling me under;
fear and dread are constant. I don't like this, Lord!

How long must I take counsel in my soul
and have sorrow in my heart all the day?
How long shall my enemy be exalted over me?

Must I stay put in this place with arrows and rocks zinging
by me?? Give me an escape route—send me
a bodyguard as I flee the careless words and
attitudes of fools, words that repulse, sting,
accuse.

*How long do you expect me—you know me!—to keep my
balance at the edge of this ledge, with the rabble
shouting senseless in every direction? I've about
had all I can take!*

This step of calling out to God honestly and fully has
been the most important step I've taken in my relationship
with God. It can be for you as well.

chapter three
asking for wisdom

Psalm 119

ALEPH

¹ Joyful are people of integrity,
who follow the instructions of the LORD.
² Joyful are those who obey his laws
and search for him with all their hearts.
³ They do not compromise with evil,
and they walk only in his paths.
⁴ You have charged us
to keep your commandments carefully.
⁵ Oh, that my actions would consistently
reflect your decrees!
⁶ Then I will not be ashamed
when I compare my life with your
commands.
⁷ As I learn your righteous regulations,
I will thank you by living as I should!

[8] I will obey your decrees.

Please don't give up on me!

I'm in college now, a small Christian college in the Midwest planted among cornfields that stretch to the horizon. It's spring break of my freshman year, and I've snagged a ride home with a guy named Duncan, who agreed to drop me off on his way to Maine. He's a fisherman from Alaska, I discover, which seems wildly improbable. How did he land here?

I soon find out I am not entirely welcome in his little Toyota Celica. The road trip was meant to be a two-person party: Duncan getting to know Janice, the campus queen. After pointing me to the back seat, where I'm wedged between stacks of luggage, Duncan drives and sends frequent admiring glances over to Janice, who keeps her gorgeous, imperious profile turned away. She all but ignores his queries, pretending interest in the fields out the window.

Soon I graduate to the passenger seat, and Janice to the back seat. Duncan asks me, "So, what's your major?"

"Umm . . . it was behavioral science, but I'm switching to English. What's yours?"

"Social science. But I'm taking all the philosophy I can. With the best professor on campus. I'm taking everything he teaches." Duncan says this with passion, hands tight on the steering wheel.

"Ohhh, philosophy! What's that about?"

Soon we are talking theology. "What are your thoughts

about foreknowledge and election?" I ask. I'm obsessed with this question. I don't know how to resolve what appears irresolvable: that God is utterly sovereign and yet that humankind has free will. At last, I've found someone as gripped by these questions as I am. We talk—heatedly, excitedly—as the miles roll beneath our tires.

"Yes, but foreknowledge and predestination aren't the same thing," Duncan insists.

"So are you a Calvinist, then? What about free will? How can God say we're responsible for our choice but then we can't choose without him?" I query, genuinely confused.

I cannot shake the topic. I have to know. I must know God rightly. The next semester I sign up for two years of Greek and as many philosophy and theology classes as I can jam into my schedule.

The next year I gain another degree, one I hadn't planned on. That Alaska fisherman proposes under an oak tree the spring of my sophomore year. Over Christmas break of my junior year, we are married.

We live happily with each other and among books. Duncan operates a bookstore in our apartment, ordering commentaries, lexicons, and Greek New Testaments at a discount for fellow students. We read all Francis Schaeffer's books; we attend conferences. We are high on doctrine and theology. Our favorite professors adopt us. Duncan and I attend dinners at their houses, discussing theology and all matters of the Christian life. I have made and found friends—even a kind of family—here.

But there are moments of sadness and confusion along the way. It is Missions Week at our college, three years from that long car conversation. We have a special speaker, the president of a mission agency. He makes frequent appearances in chapel and is well known in the student body. We call him "Weeping Wally" for his tendency to break out into dramatic sobs during his messages.

This week goes as expected, with many teary missionary stories. Now it's Friday, the final night, the close of the whole conference. All two thousand students—the entire student body—are here, as required. The organ begins a familiar drone. The pianist takes her place beside the stage and adds some higher chords.

The mission director grips the pulpit now with fresh purpose. He's already sweating and florid from his message. He blots his face. "It's time to make a decision, ladies and gentlemen." He turns, making deliberate eye contact with every section of the auditorium. "This week, you've heard about the desperate needs around the world. The world is lost and dying and going to hell. The fields are white unto harvest, but workers are few. Will you go? Will you be the one that brings the light to the dark places of the world?" He speaks forcefully, his voice rising and cracking with emotion. "Close your eyes now; bow your heads. We're going to sing 'Just as I Am,' and we're going to let the Lord have his way with us."

I dutifully bow my head and sing softly the words I know by heart: "Just as I am without one plea / but that thy blood was shed for me / and that thou bidst me come to thee."[1] I had sung it with my youth group at every rally and event through my high school years. Those words had tugged me forward down the aisle to ask for forgiveness and salvation again and again.

Halfway through the second verse, though, no one in the audience has stirred. He begins again.

"The Lord is calling you. Do you hear it?" he booms with more intensity. "Come on down the aisle and say, 'Yes, Lord, I hear you! I want to go!' Who will come?"

The organ and piano moan through the second verse. No one moves. Two thousand of us are locked in place, only our lips moving to the verses. So he begins a succession of callouts, first to sports teams: "Do you hear God calling you? People are dying, lost, out on the mission field and you're playing basketball!" Then he moves to musicians, then on to Bible majors. To my surprise, by the sixth verse he's down to English majors, my tribe, which I know is scraping the bottom of the missionary barrel. But I'm sad and frustrated at his theology, at this clear assumption that the only sacred work is "full-time Christian service." Doesn't he know that all life and work belong to Christ, all life and work can be sacred?

His cries get louder, his face redder. A handful of students shuffle guiltily down the gold-carpeted aisle.

"Close your eyes and bow your heads one last time," he directs. His voice is still commanding, but now there's a tinge of anxiety. "We're not leaving here until God has his way.

Now, one final time, with your eyes closed, God is calling you to full-time Christian service. To go to the mission field wherever he calls. Will you go? Will you go? If you're saying yes, just slip your hand up right where you are. No one can see but me. Just slip your hand up and I'll pray for you. Who is answering God's call?"

We stand under the intensifying tearful barrage for twenty more minutes. Apparently, if the Holy Spirit isn't doing his job, someone else has to. Finally, realizing there is no other way to end the service, a few more people stumble down the aisle.

Duncan and I are deeply grieved about the evening performance. We write a letter to the speaker, questioning his theology and guilt-based methodology.

Four days later we are called before the college president, who is angry. Unless we write a letter of apology, we will be expelled without our degrees.

When I first chose to follow Jesus, I had no idea how many different voices would divide the Psalm 1 path into multiple, narrower lanes. One stands by the outmost lane, calling: "Know God through your mind!" Another shouts on the other side: "No, it's here! God speaks through your emotions!" And another: "God speaks through *me!*"

Nor did I expect so many off-ramps along that path, and they seem to multiply year by year. This week a friend writes me to say he is deconstructing all he was taught in church and has found that there's nothing left. A whole generation of people are joining him. We are watching Christian leaders—famous for their knowledge, their charismatic teaching, their books—plummet from their platforms as their secret lives are exposed. We're hearing Christian musicians and celebrity pastors proclaim they don't believe in Jesus anymore. Other friends are speaking a whole new faith language, immersed in a religion of politics.

How does this happen?

At the very beginnings of our human story, we learn that we are a people tempted to heed the wrong voice. Eve holds in her hand the luscious fruit, the serpent's voice in her ear. At the base of the very mountain where God meets with Moses, voices insist on creating and worshiping a golden calf. The Israelites believe the voices of ten frightened men, refusing to enter the Promised Land God is giving them, though he has promised them victory; they will wander in the desert for forty years, one year for every day they distrusted Yahweh.

Weeping Wally's pleas and the college president's ultimatum were deeply disappointing finales to my college years. Neither marked the end of disappointments and confusions in my faith life.

But the path is still there in front of us. Do you see? Our God is not silent, leaving us to riddle and muddle our way along. He has spoken. In the middle of this book of a thousand pages, with so many stories and songs and words from the pen of man and the very heart of God, wisdom waits. The voice of wisdom calls. All the wisdom psalms in the prayer book of the church are powerful, but one wisdom psalm in particular calls me back again and again: Psalm 119.

Psalm 119 is also known as a Torah psalm, with the word *torah* (most often translated "teaching" or "law") appearing twenty-five times. This is the longest psalm in the entire collection and the longest chapter in all of God's Word. And I find it one of the most stunning conversations between humans and God. Listen to how it starts:

How happy are those whose way is blameless,
 who live according to the LORD's instruction!
Happy are those who keep His decrees
 and seek Him with all their heart.[2]

Do you hear it? We're back at the gate of Psalm 1, which is also a wisdom psalm and a Torah psalm. Do you want to live a happy and blameless life? Then live by God's words! Seek him with everything you've got!

But then Psalm 119 introduces us to a problem that Psalm 1 doesn't mention:

You have laid down precepts
 that are to be fully obeyed.
Oh, that my ways were steadfast
 in obeying your decrees![3]

God's Word brings delight and blessing and soul-prosperity, but we are not steadfast. We waver, we waffle, we wander, and the psalmist does too. In the 176 verses of this extraordinary psalm-prayer, he takes us down those winding paths:

> I am a stranger on earth;
>> do not hide Your commands from me.[4]

> Keep me from lying to myself;
>> give me the privilege of knowing your
>> instructions.[5]

> You made me; you created me.
>> Now give me the sense to follow your
>> commands.[6]

> How long must I wait?
>> When will you punish those who
>> persecute me?[7]

> Argue my case; take my side!
>> Protect my life as you promised.[8]

So we can't trust ourselves. We can't trust our circumstances. We're embattled and exhausted. How can we be wise, then? How can we stay on the Godward path?

The writer of Psalm 119, who many believe is King David, helps us see the answer by doing something remarkable in the craft of the poem itself. Psalm 119 is an intricate alphabet acrostic. Each stanza of eight lines is built around a Hebrew letter. As we make our way through the psalm, the stanzas take us all the way from A to Z, signifying wholeness. The Word of God is complete, comprehensive, sufficient for every circumstance of life, from beginning to end. To make sure the reader and the hearer get this, every first word in each line begins with the letter of that stanza.

Already, as a poet who struggles with writing in form, I am astounded at this complexity. Yet there's more. In nearly every line of Psalm 119, the poet references God's written Word. Each time he does, he chooses from one of eight Hebrew words. So within each eight-line stanza, eight different Hebrew words may be employed, each focusing on a slightly different aspect of God's Word.

What is the purpose of all this structure? As the psalmist makes his way through the alphabet, through the A to Z of his life experiences, he is tethering himself to God's Word. In one breath, the psalmist is persecuted. In the next, he prays for God's truth. One moment, he's lonely. In the next, he turns to the company of God's instructions. He's afflicted. He looks with hope to God's promises.

For all its astonishing intricacy, this psalm is more than an exercise in wordsmithing; it's about loving and attaching to God. Crafting these stanzas and couplets would take time, careful thought, and prayer. It's possible that Psalm 119 was composed over a long period as a kind of prayer journal. Perhaps the psalmist wrote just one verse a day. Perhaps he wrote over an entire year, or even his entire lifetime! In other words, the psalmist would have had to meditate day and night on God's Word and God's character to create this finely sculpted poem.

But the balanced parallel lines and the sound patterns serve another purpose as well. The psalms were not a document to study silently in the Temple; they were prayer-songs to be sung, taught, and passed on aloud. The mnemonic devices allowed for easier memorization. These words were meant to be planted and then enacted from the heart, soul, and mind for a lifetime.

What would happen when God's people did this? What kind of people would they become? Moses tells them—and he speaks to us as well:

Look, I have taught you statutes and ordinances as the LORD my God has commanded me, so that you may follow them in the land you are entering to possess. Carefully follow them, for this will show your wisdom and understanding in the eyes of the peoples. When they hear about all these statutes, they will say, 'This great nation is indeed a wise and understanding people.' *For what great nation is there that has a god near to it as the LORD our God is to us whenever we call to Him?*[9]

The writer of Psalm 119 ends up there as well. After a month or a year or a lifetime of composing this prayer journal, this God-seeker ends up in this poignant, extraordinary place:

I have wandered away like a lost sheep;
come and find me,
for I have not forgotten your commands.[10]

I believe that the writer of Psalm 119 is modeling a powerful path into God's Word and God's way. Our God has spoken, and he has given us the power of language in turn so that we may shape and mold our desires, our walk, our path. In these prayers, God's people are not simply reading or singing aloud about God—they are bringing themselves before the throne and the face of God. As they experience the loving presence of God, they are making promises, commitments, intentional choices to speak and embody the teachings of God and walk along the Psalm 1 path.

When we take on this practice and follow this model, we are doing the same. Through every life circumstance, we are attaching ourselves to our Father, the source of all wisdom, truth, and love. And before his face we are setting our intentions to turn away from all other paths and alluring voices, to follow his words and his ways alone.

How then can we make it through the noisy voices and forked paths before us each day? We abandon our self-sufficiency, all our own means of accruing knowledge and determining rightness. We turn to God's Word and follow the poet's lead: "Yahweh, come and find us!"

■ draw near

Highlights of Psalm 119

· The longest psalm and longest chapter in the Bible.

· An alphabet acrostic with twenty-two stanzas, each built on a successive letter of the alphabet.

· Each stanza is composed of eight verses, each verse beginning with the same letter.

· Nearly every verse references one of eight Hebrew words for God's teachings.

· A love letter to God and the power of his Word.

· The carefully crafted structure illustrates how God's wisdom and teachings bring order, design, and beauty to the disorder of our lives.

· The careful artistry of the psalm reveals the writer's deep commitment to spending time with God and his Word.

The New Testament book of James encourages us, "If any of you lacks wisdom, let him ask God."[11] If you need to hear from God, if you're seeking wisdom for a particular decision, writing into the wisdom psalms is a marvelous way to bring this before him.

Wisdom Psalms[12]

Psalms 1, 37, 49, 73, 91, 112, 119, 128, 133

In our practice, we're going to approach Psalm 119 with the spirit in which it was written: actively seeking God and his wisdom. Before we do, let's remember our acronym for entering into prayer through the Psalms:

NEARING

- **N**otate (Write out the original psalm by hand, an action that uses both sides of the brain.)
- **E**xpress (Use your voice and body gestures/movements to give full expression to the psalm.)
- **A**mplify (Add your response/circumstance/witness to the psalm.)
- **R**ead (Understand the original psalm in its context, reading different versions if desired.)
- **I**dentify (Personalize the psalm to you and/or to your faith community.)
- **N**ew Testament Fulfillment (Add relevant New Testament verses that augment and fulfill the message of the psalm.)
- **G**ather (Share psalm-prayers in worship with your faith community.)

We can experience the wisdom and teaching of this psalm for ourselves in four ways: **Read**, **Notate**, **Amplify**, and **Express**.

Read

Read as much of Psalm 119 as you're able to right now. Of the twenty-two stanzas, I've included six here, chosen for their range of expression and circumstances. But it's worth the time to at least peruse the psalm in its entirety. (My favorite translations are the NLT, used here, and *The Message*.) Notice how intensely personal the psalm is: It's written in the first person throughout, and it directly addresses God with a range of poignant pleas. As you're reading, choose one or two stanzas that speak to you particularly.

Psalm 119

ALEPH

¹ Joyful are people of integrity,
   who follow the instructions of the LORD.
² Joyful are those who obey his laws
   and search for him with all their
      hearts.
³ They do not compromise with evil,
   and they walk only in his paths.
⁴ You have charged us
   to keep your commandments carefully.
⁵ Oh, that my actions would consistently
   reflect your decrees!
⁶ Then I will not be ashamed
   when I compare my life with your commands.
⁷ As I learn your righteous regulations,
   I will thank you by living as I should!

[8] I will obey your decrees.
    Please don't give up on me!

BETH

[9] How can a young person stay pure?
    By obeying your word.
[10] I have tried hard to find you—
    don't let me wander from your
        commands.
[11] I have hidden your word in my heart,
    that I might not sin against you.
[12] I praise you, O LORD;
    teach me your decrees.
[13] I have recited aloud
    all the regulations you have given us.
[14] I have rejoiced in your laws
    as much as in riches.
[15] I will study your commandments
    and reflect on your ways.
[16] I will delight in your decrees
    and not forget your word.

DALETH

[25] I lie in the dust;
    revive me by your word.
[26] I told you my plans, and you answered.
    Now teach me your decrees.
[27] Help me understand the meaning of your commandments,

and I will meditate on your wonderful deeds.
28 I weep with sorrow;
   encourage me by your word.
29 Keep me from lying to myself;
   give me the privilege of knowing your instructions.
30 I have chosen to be faithful;
   I have determined to live by your regulations.
31 I cling to your laws.
   LORD, don't let me be put to shame!
32 I will pursue your commands,
   for you expand my understanding.

TETH

65 You have done many good things for me, LORD,
   just as you promised.
66 I believe in your commands;
   now teach me good judgment and knowledge.
67 I used to wander off until you disciplined me;
   but now I closely follow your word.
68 You are good and do only good;
   teach me your decrees.
69 Arrogant people smear me with lies,
   but in truth I obey your commandments with all my heart.
70 Their hearts are dull and stupid,
   but I delight in your instructions.
71 My suffering was good for me,
   for it taught me to pay attention to your decrees.
72 Your instructions are more valuable to me
   than millions in gold and silver.

LAMEDH

⁸⁹ Your eternal word, O Lord,

stands firm in heaven.

⁹⁰ Your faithfulness extends to every generation,

as enduring as the earth you created.

⁹¹ Your regulations remain true to this day,

for everything serves your plans.

⁹² If your instructions hadn't sustained me with joy,

I would have died in my misery.

⁹³ I will never forget your commandments,

for by them you give me life.

⁹⁴ I am yours; rescue me!

For I have worked hard at obeying your

commandments.

⁹⁵ Though the wicked hide along the way to kill me,

I will quietly keep my mind on your laws.

⁹⁶ Even perfection has its limits,

but your commands have no limit.

TAW

¹⁶⁹ O Lord, listen to my cry;

give me the discerning mind you promised.

¹⁷⁰ Listen to my prayer;

rescue me as you promised.

¹⁷¹ Let praise flow from my lips,

for you have taught me your decrees.

¹⁷² Let my tongue sing about your word,

for all your commands are right.

[173] Give me a helping hand,
   for I have chosen to follow your commandments.
[174] O LORD, I have longed for your rescue,
   and your instructions are my delight.
[175] Let me live so I can praise you,
   and may your regulations help me.
[176] I have wandered away like a lost sheep;
   come and find me,
   for I have not forgotten your commands.

Notate

Write out by hand the stanzas you have chosen. (Remember, this helps us use both sides of the brain.) Leave two or three lines of space below each verse for the next activity. Alternately, you can write the stanza on the left side of the page, leaving the right side for your own stanza.

Amplify

There are several fruitful ways to **Amplify** these verses, creating your own psalm-prayer for wisdom.

1. Paraphrase each verse in your own words, staying as close as possible to the meaning of the original.

2. Follow the movement and sense of each verse, but rather than speaking generally, address your request and circumstances more specifically.

   For example:

O LORD, I have longed for your rescue,
and your instructions are my delight.[13]

Dear Lord, I wait for your rescue every day at work,
and while I wait, it's your Word that I read during
lunch that brings me joy.

3. For the adventurous, compose one stanza that follows the original acrostic pattern of this psalm. (This is fun to do with a friend or in a group.) Choose a stanza that's particularly powerful to you. Then choose the letter that each verse will start with. (Hint: *R, L, B,* and *P* are good letters to use.) As you paraphrase each line, stay as close as possible to the meaning. (Don't let the challenge and fun of this exercise reduce God's Word to a puzzle or a literary art object. Instead, allow this exercise to give you a fresh, hands-on appreciation for the intensive artistry of an acrostic psalm as you draw nearer to God.)

Express

When you have finished your psalm-prayer, read or sing your prayer aloud to God. Let your body move into whatever gestures or postures arise from your words. If you are seeking God's help, consider raising your hands, open, before the Lord.

A prayer labyrinth can be a helpful way of embodying the process of a wisdom psalm-prayer. A labyrinth can take several different forms, but it's often a circular path that the pray-er walks slowly, meditatively, from the outer circle to the center of the circle, which represents the presence of God. If you have access to a labyrinth, you can walk it as you pray, using Psalm 119 or another wisdom psalm as you go, pausing when needed to meditate or go over a current dilemma. If an established labyrinth is not available, simply walk slowly in a large circle or a figure-eight path in the yard or a room, allowing for whatever postures feel organic to the text or the meditation.

God speaks to us, and we to him, so that we can know and experience one another, can draw close. The greatest wisdom imparted in this wisdom psalm is how desperately we need God and how present and ready God is to hear and respond. Our Father loves to hear from his children!

resting in trust

Psalm 23 (NIV)
A PSALM OF DAVID

¹The LORD is my shepherd, I lack nothing.
²He makes me lie down in green
     pastures,
  he leads me beside quiet waters,
³he refreshes my soul.
He guides me along the right paths
  for his name's sake.
⁴Even though I walk
  through the darkest valley,
I will fear no evil,
  for you are with me;
your rod and your staff,
  they comfort me.

⁵You prepare a table before me
  in the presence of my enemies.

You anoint my head with oil;
   my cup overflows.
   [6] Surely your goodness and love will follow me
   all the days of my life,
and I will dwell in the house of the LORD
   forever.

It is morning. The dull light illuminates our tiny loft. I stir, feel for Duncan beside me in our double bed. He is already up and out. I check my watch. It's seven fifteen. I creak my young but weary body out of the army blankets. We didn't get in from the fishing nets until eleven thirty last night, like the night before and the one before that. I am sore all over and aching for more sleep. I take three steps across the loft, reach into the wooden crate that serves as our dresser. I pull on jeans, a sweatshirt, knee boots. I think I'm awake, but I'm not sure. I turn around and climb down the ladder to the workshop below.

It's my first summer in Alaska, on a forty-acre island off Kodiak Island. I'm a fisherman now. Or rather, I'm trying to be a fisherman, like my new husband, who has done this all his life. I'm on board for this, loving a challenge and, even more, loving the wild, raw seascape that is now my summer home. But this week I am struggling.

Stiff and slow, I climb the grassy hill to the little red cabin where through the window I see everyone else already gathered around the table. This is the three-room cabin that

Duncan and his brothers grew up in. The blue door rasps open. I tread as lightly as I can, entering the tiny living room that also serves as the dining room and the everything room. Now it's the breakfast room.

Wanda, my mother-in-law, is just setting down a plate of hot biscuits. She turns and smiles at me.

"Sorry I'm late, everyone."

"How did you sleep, my dear?" Dewitt, my father-in-law, smiles at me from the end of the table.

"Pretty good!" I duck into my seat between Duncan and his brother.

Dewitt has his Bible open in front of him. He's eyeing the plate of hot biscuits, and I realize everyone has waited for me. And is waiting now for Dewitt to read.

"We're on Psalm 23 this mornin'," Dewitt drawls. "I think everyone knows this one." And he begins to read the familiar words in his raspy voice and Oklahoma accent: "The Lord is my shepherd."

At my first breakfast with my new family on this faraway island, my father-in-law announced, "Well, we're gonna read a psalm a day here in the mornin'. That's a good way to start the day." If we're on Psalm 23, then I've been here at least that many days.

That first day, I would have preferred if he had chosen Galatians or Hebrews. But something in me is changing. I am five thousand miles away from New Hampshire now, four thousand away from college. I'm no longer living in the pages of books or debating theology with Duncan. On this tiny, treeless island, surrounded by fur and feathers and the flash of salmon and the sky-high spouts of leviathans, I am beginning to glimpse the vastness and wildness of the God I've been studying. And I am beginning to see that this island is not an easy or a safe place to live.

A couple of weeks pass. Now, late at night in an eighteen-foot wooden skiff, I am on one of our fishing nets alone. We always work in pairs, but this week has turned our "always" into whatever is needed. Tonight, my boat is heavy in the water with too many salmon.

Are we crazy for doing this? This salmon season, there are only five of us running nine long nets around the island. And now the run of salmon has come, and we cannot keep up. After two weeks of little sleep, with my two hands picking and pitching a thousand salmon every day, little of me is left. Duncan has gone in another skiff to finish another net, leaving me here alone near dark to finish extracting the final fish.

I have no one to appeal to. We are cut off from the outside world, connected only by letters we retrieve from the post office in an hour-long boat ride once a week. How can I complain even in letters to my mother, who was unhappy that I chose to live a world away? I feel profoundly alone.

I rest for a few short seconds, leaning on the skiff sides and catching my breath after pulling in a tangle of a dozen salmon. The waters of the Gulf of Alaska gently rock the boat. I hear an engine and turn. Out of the dark, I see the glow of a skiff's bow, this boat as heavy in the water as mine.

Duncan. It's too dark to see his face, but I recognize his white fishing hat. He throttles down and slows parallel to my skiff. "Leslie! We're done! Can you take the skiff to the tender?" He's running his boat alone too.

My stomach flips. I've only run a boat a few times. But in the dark with a load of fish? I hesitate.

"Leslie, you have to take it," he says with urgency. "We can just make it through the spit if you hurry. Otherwise, you'll have to go all the way around the island. Just follow me! I'll give you a minute to unhook the net, and then just follow my wake."

"Okay!" I shout back reluctantly. I know there's no other way. But I am scared. The spit is a series of boulders across a sand peninsula with just one clear path through. The passage is narrow, and if you miscalculate, you slam into a boulder or hit the hidden rocks just below the water.

I unhook the net from the boat, let it drop back into the water, then wait for the wind to push me away from the webbing. Once I've drifted past, I release the forty-horse outboard back into the water, pull the cord vigorously two times, three times; on the fourth it roars to life, and I am off under my own power in this Alaskan night.

Because I can see so little, I hear everything. The ocean slapping my skiff, the engine, Duncan's engine ahead of me. There's a moon up there somewhere, pressed dim against the clouds, giving just enough light for me to catch the white of Duncan's wake ahead of me. My night vision has always been poor, and now in the dark I am captain of a tiny boat I barely know how to run. I stand in the stern, eyes afire over the skiff's bow, feet and legs absorbing the rocking of the boat. I want to trade places with anyone else right now, especially one of my friends in college sitting calmly, easily in a chair, taking notes from a theology professor. But here I am, trying not to run the skiff into a rock, or lose the fish, or die.

"Help me, Lord," I say over the din of the engine and the waves. And, unbidden, the words come: *The Lord is my shepherd.* I see the words, see in my mind a shadowy figure ahead of me. *I shall not want.* I don't want anything right now but his presence beside me. *He makes me to lie down in green pastures. He leads me beside quiet waters. He restores my soul.*

I see a flash of white on my right. No, not Duncan—that's the outer part of the reef. I throttle down, steer away. There are boulders on the other side, too. My stomach clenches and I lean forward farther. I hear Duncan's engine still, then— there! I see the wake again.

Yea, though I walk through the valley of the shadow of death. I don't know if I am saying this under my breath or out loud, but I hear the words in my body clearly. *I will fear no evil. For your rod and your staff comfort me.* Now I see white on both sides of me, I hear the sucking and gurgling of water against the rocks. I am just feet away from them on both sides. I am holding my breath, I slow to nearly stopping; my own wake urges me forward now through the strait. *You prepare a table before me in the presence of my enemies.*

I am through now, the last rock six feet away on my right. I remember where it is. I throttle up carefully, eyes ahead on

Duncan, who is now approaching the tender, the larger boat that will take our fish. The lights of the boat blind me but look like the lights of heaven. *My cup runneth over.* Soon my fish are pitched and delivered, the skiff is tied to the running line, and I am on the path up the hill to our bed in the loft. The words trail behind me like my own wake in the night: *Surely goodness and mercy shall follow me all the days of my life.* Then, up the ladder to our loft—*And I will dwell in the house of the Lord forever.* And I will try to sleep.

I memorized this psalm years ago and did not think about it while in college. But here, in this untamed place, surrounded by uncertainty and danger, the words come back to me. Not the Ten Commandments, though I know how essential they are to life and living. Not the Nicene Creed or the Apostles' Creed, though I treasure their truths. I did not sit there, mind swirling, body shaking, reciting the attributes of God: "God is omnipotent, omniscient, omnipresent. God exists as a Trinity: Father, Son, Holy Ghost."

Instead, these lines of poetry met me in the dark.

Psalm 23 was one of the first passages of Scripture I memorized. That summer and for years to come, I would speak those words again and again. So have many others through the centuries. Out of all the thousand pages in the Scriptures, this one poem-song is perhaps the most known and beloved.

Psalm 23 is categorized as a trust psalm. Who does not need this? Who does not live with uncertainty, fear, apprehension? Aren't we all heavy-laden, feeling and finding our way in the dark, sometimes with little but the flash of the wake before us to lead us onward? A friend dies, a husband leaves the marriage, a house burns in a wildfire, a daughter has cancer, work overwhelms. We are disoriented, dislocated. We are not at home in our bodies, our families, even in our homes anymore.

Often in this disruption we lose language as well. We don't know how to speak or what to say to get back home, to orient ourselves to this new reality. What we want and need most in our dislocation is to know the end of the story.

Trust psalms take us there. They build a linguistic bridge from the trouble we experience to the God we believe is near and ready to help. Along the winding, shadowed path of our lives, trust psalms remind us that God will always lead us home.

Psalm 121, another trust psalm, ends with this reality:

> The LORD is your shade at your right hand;
> the sun will not harm you by day,
>   nor the moon by night.
> The LORD will keep you from all harm—
>   he will watch over your life;
> the LORD will watch over your coming and going
>   both now and forevermore.[1]

Can we truly believe in God's nearness and presence, his watchful protection and care? Are these words just a naive hope?

Surely David himself must have questioned and wondered.

I can almost see him in his study, further along in years, facing trouble in his kingdom. Again. Threats and upstarts, invading armies and wars. Rebellions from within, even sons who want to displace him. People who care nothing for the loving rule of Yahweh. He is filled with emotion, trepidation, anxiety as he faces yet another crisis.

But lament is not what he needs right now.

His mind flashes back to his shepherding days. The lush meadows! That gentle brook running slow and silent. The sheep trusting him utterly, following him everywhere!

How he loved the sheep, even as a boy. His protection was fierce—he fought off a bear, a lion. His body remembers. His muscles remember.

And he sees, too, how God has led him, shepherded him through all the years: facing Goliath, evading the spear and sword of King Saul, fighting the Philistines . . . He sees how God has led him in his role as king as he labored to shepherd the people of Israel, who were so like the sheep of his boyhood. And truly, he realizes it now: He has never needed anything but Yahweh himself.

Looking back gives David strength and confidence for what lies ahead. He doesn't know this exact story's end, but he knows the God who guides the end. Through all the battles, he's experienced again and again the *hesed* love of God.

The psalmists use this word *hesed* more than a hundred times. There's no perfect English equivalent, though translators have used "lovingkindness," "steadfast love," and "unfailing love" to try to get close.

We hear *hesed* from the very mouth of God just before he establishes the covenant with Moses and the Hebrew people. God passes before Moses and proclaims these truths about himself:

> "The LORD, the LORD, the compassionate and gracious God, slow to anger, abounding in *hesed* and faithfulness, maintaining *hesed* to thousands, and forgiving wickedness, rebellion, and sin . . ."[2]

And so, with his mind's eye ablaze, David remembers Yahweh's covenant-keeping love. He sits, writes, crafts this song:

> The LORD is my shepherd. . . .
> He leads me beside quiet waters,
>   he refreshes my soul.[3]

Why are these simple words so powerful? There's beauty and simplicity in the language, yes—but the metaphor paints an image we cannot forget.

The Psalms overflow with metaphor, from the opening psalm to the last. What are my enemies? They are strong bulls.[4] They are roaring lions.[5] Who is my God? God is an immovable and steady rock, an unassailable fortress.[6] God is a shield.[7] God is our shade.[8] God is my shepherd.

As we reach out tremulous hands to God, we're not left to hitch our anxieties to an abstract idea. Metaphor connects one thing to another, often coupling the intangible to the known, the invisible to the visible. Metaphor leads us to the deeper truth that our God draws near to us in the world we inhabit. In our need, he doesn't reach down two airy arms to save our feathery souls and then abandon our bodies to fight the lions. God comes to us as a father to a child, as a mother to an infant, as a shield to those in battle, as a tower to those on the flooded plains, as a radiant light in the pitch of night, as the soft, cool shade in the desert sun.

A thousand years after David, Jesus would identify himself through a host of metaphors: He is the Good Shepherd, the Bread of Life, the Vine, the Light of the World, the Lamb. He called the Passover bread his body, the wine his blood. God names himself—and we name him too—through the bodies and things of this world. This is Immanuel, our Creator who is not far from us but near, a God who is with us in the muck and fire and storm.

Poetry, memory, and metaphor guide us down the path to trust. If we're going to "taste and see that the LORD is good,"[9] we are going to need more than abstract knowledge about God. God has given each of us a memory, a sensory-rich brain and body to perceive him in our own particular world—and in the midst of that world, to trust him.

■ draw near

Don't we need these comforting words and truths? Don't we all long to find our way to solid ground? Even when we feel distant from God, these prayer-songs can guide us through the dark. We can look back and discover some of the ways God has been present throughout our lives. And we can learn language to call him into our difficult present, to find rest in his promises.

In our practice, we're going to dig into two trust psalms, each one full of imagery, metaphor, and the utmost confidence in God's *hesed* love, his unfailing love. Before we do, let's remember our acronym for entering into prayer through the Psalms:

NEARING

- **N**otate (Write out the original psalm by hand, an action that uses both sides of the brain.)
- **E**xpress (Use your voice and body gestures/movements to give full expression to the psalm.)
- **A**mplify (Add your response/circumstance/witness to the psalm.)
- **R**ead (Understand the original psalm in its context, reading different versions if desired.)
- **I**dentify (Personalize the psalm to you and/or to your faith community.)
- **N**ew Testament Fulfillment (Add relevant New Testament verses that augment and fulfill the message of the psalm.)
- **G**ather (Share psalm-prayers in worship with your faith community.)

As we write into this first trust psalm, our own remembrances of God's acts and graces in our lives, along with the truths of their metaphors and imagery, will tuck us, anxieties and all, safely under the wings of God. We can do this alone, but gathering and sharing our psalms with one another adds a fuller measure of joy and communion. We will step into trust in these ways: **Amplify**, **Gather**, and **Express**.

1. Let's start with an exercise that reveals the power of poetry and metaphor. Look at Psalm 23. Write each line out simply, removing all poetic language. For example:

   God leads me.
   I don't need anything.

2. What is lost without metaphor?

Amplify

Choose a metaphor from your own life. Psalm 23 hinges on an extended metaphor, but it's more than that. It's also a story—a story of the pilgrim life: where it wends and winds, how God has been present, and finally where it all ends up. As you contemplate a metaphor for your prayer, consider the following questions: How have you experienced the care and leading of God? What has God been like throughout your life, or even throughout this last year?

Here are some examples of personalized metaphors:

- Linda, who has worked in remote places around the world as a nurse to leprosy patients, writes: "The Lord is my wound-dresser."

- Laurie, a writer, pens: "The Lord is my author."

- Judy, a dancer, writes: "The Lord is my dance partner."

As we explore metaphor in our prayers, please remember, we are not rewriting Scripture, nor are we renaming God. We are following David's example, finding language to connect us to God as we describe through imagery and metaphor his character and his personal care for us. As we do this, we'll encounter God in our past, in our autobiographical memory.

Write your own Psalm 23. The pattern of the psalm can guide you as you write your prayer:

The Lord is my _____

Where has he brought me? _____

_____

How has he tended me? _____

How has he led me through troubled times? _____

_____

_____

Why am I not afraid? _____

_____

How does he bring me assurance? _____

_____

How does he bring me assurance despite trouble? _____
_____

Where will he bring me, finally? _____
_____

How does he bring me assurance at the end of my life? ____
_____
_____

Here's how my Psalm 23 has unfolded:

Leslie's Psalm 23
The Lord captains me.
I in my boat on high seas
See him standing with me
As I steer. I shall be calm.
He will still the waves,
Still me.
The sting of the jellyfish,
The bite of the shark,
The scream of the wind—none
Of this shall pain.
Surely goodness and fish
Will fill my boat
All the summers of my life.
And after, I will come ashore to live
In the cabin of the Lord
Forever.

Gather and Express

Share your psalm aloud with others, taking turns reading in a circle. Let your body find its own physical expression of your words. Here are some suggestions to get you started:

- Breathe deeply throughout this exercise. Let your arms hang loosely at your side, palms forward, face raised heavenward. Sway back and forth, playing with your sense of balance.

- Settle into a solid and grounded shape. Be aware of the stability of your stance.

- Finish with a circular gesture depicting God's unending love and presence.

Psalm 91 is a longer psalm, with sixteen verses, but every verse creates a poetic portrait of God's personal deliverance of his beloved ones. Even more noteworthy, in the final verses God himself speaks directly to us, uttering promises we can cling to no matter our circumstances. Because of this, I suggest that we do less alteration of this psalm. As we engage this psalm, we will focus on **Notate**, **Identify**, and **Express**.

1. If you have time, **Notate** the entire psalm. If you have less time, write out the verses that speak particularly to your life right now. We need to be wary of wrenching verses or passages of Scripture out of context and applying them to ourselves. However, because this entire psalm expresses one central idea, we can reliably interact with shorter sections.

2. As you **Notate**, you can **Identify** at the same time: switching the second-person *you* and *your* to first-person *I, me,* and *my*. This will help you hear and more fully grasp the assurances God is giving you.

3. **Express** your psalm-prayer through body and voice to the Lord, your refuge and fortress.

Psalm 91 (ESV)

¹ He who dwells in the shelter of the Most High
      will abide in the shadow of the Almighty.
² I will say to the LORD, "My refuge and my fortress,
      my God, in whom I trust."

³ For he will deliver you from the snare of
            the fowler
      and from the deadly pestilence.
⁴ He will cover you with his pinions,
      and under his wings you will find refuge;
      his faithfulness is a shield and buckler.
⁵ You will not fear the terror of the night,
      nor the arrow that flies by day,
⁶ nor the pestilence that stalks in darkness,
      nor the destruction that wastes at noonday.

⁷ A thousand may fall at your side,
      ten thousand at your right hand,
      but it will not come near you.

⁸ You will only look with your eyes
        and see the recompense of the wicked.

⁹ Because you have made the LORD your
            dwelling place—
        the Most High, who is my refuge—
¹⁰ no evil shall be allowed to befall you,
        no plague come near your tent.

¹¹ For he will command his angels
            concerning you
        to guard you in all your ways.
¹² On their hands they will bear you up,
        lest you strike your foot against a stone.
¹³ You will tread on the lion and the adder;
        the young lion and the serpent you will
            trample underfoot.

¹⁴ "Because he holds fast to me in love,
        I will deliver him;
    I will protect him, because he knows
        my name.
¹⁵ When he calls to me, I will answer him;
        I will be with him in trouble;
    I will rescue him and honor him.
¹⁶ With long life I will satisfy him
        and show him my salvation."

Discovering God in our past will reveal his presence in our present, strengthening our trust to reach all the way to our furthest future. We can know now for sure: God will always lead us home.

Trust Psalms[10]

Psalms 4, 11, 16, 23, 27 (verses 1-6), 62, 91, 121, 125, 131

chapter five
being honest in confession

Psalm 51

FOR THE CHOIR DIRECTOR: A PSALM OF DAVID, REGARDING THE TIME NATHAN
THE PROPHET CAME TO HIM AFTER DAVID HAD COMMITTED ADULTERY WITH
BATHSHEBA.

¹Have mercy on me, O God,
   because of your unfailing love.
Because of your great compassion,
   blot out the stain of my sins.
²Wash me clean from my guilt.
   Purify me from my sin.
³For I recognize my rebellion;
   it haunts me day and night.
⁴Against you, and you alone, have I sinned;
   I have done what is evil in your sight.
You will be proved right in what you say,
   and your judgment against me is just.
⁵For I was born a sinner—
   yes, from the moment my mother conceived me.

⁶ But you desire honesty from the womb,
  teaching me wisdom even there.

⁷ Purify me from my sins, and I will be clean;
  wash me, and I will be whiter than snow.
⁸ Oh, give me back my joy again;
  you have broken me—
  now let me rejoice.

Duncan and I leave our summer fishing lives behind each winter for graduate studies at the University of Oregon. I'm in the middle of a master's program in literature now, having just finished one in journalism. Duncan is in law school. We don't know what we'll do with these degrees. We don't have a plan. We only know we love to learn, and we have so much more to learn. We'll be here for three years, in between summers on the island. We're in classes every day. We go to church. We think of ourselves as faithful believers. But I am struggling.

Ocean storms have given way to midterms. This crisp spring day, I'm on my way to a blue-book exam in my medieval literature class, which means two or three essay questions, lengthy, argued responses, and a thorough understanding of the medieval worldview. The professor wears his hair in a tonsure like a twelfth-century monk and is openly disdainful of students who don't meet his expectations. I have read all the literature. I have studied, written papers, passed an oral exam reciting the *Canterbury Tales* in Middle English. I have an A- right now. Getting a B in this program is considered a failure.

I'm grateful to be in this program, but I'm sure everyone else is smarter than me. What right do I have to be here among these brilliant professors and students who move and speak with such assurance? I cannot forget who I really am, where I have come from: the loveless, deconstructed houses of my past; the violence of the village school we were trapped in; the tiny Christian college that my professors and peers here would scorn. And now the Alaskan island where I disappear every summer, hands sunk in fish instead of books. After this exam I'll be fully exposed.

But my steps are heavy with an added weight. Walking toward campus and the final exam propels me toward another summer on the island. We'll be there on the rocky shores, thrown into the centrifuge of fishing, in less than two weeks. One series of exams measuring my worth followed by another. I'm not sure I can do it again. Every summer is more challenging than the last. In the middle of last summer, I tried to leave, escaping for a few days down a long beach, staying in a deserted driftwood shack.

My steps slow and drag now, my chest begins to hurt. I approach the corner slowly, then stand on the curb as the cars tear past, pulling my skirt after them. I have a sudden urge to run, the way I'd run into the woods as a child, the way I ran across the spit to flee the island. But I'm torn. Should I run out in front of the cars, or should I follow behind them, out of the city and into an easier life? I stand for what feels like hours, as if either one is a legitimate choice. Then the light turns red, the cars stop, I take a deep breath and steer my feet across the street. I'm tired of dread.

After the exam, I walk home, thinking of that corner, thinking of the longing to run and feeling shocked and ashamed. Even in my fear of failure, I feel like a failure. I try to pray, though I hardly know what to say. Then I think of David. I remember his failures, and I feel a surge of hope. Our stories are not the same, but I see myself there.

Though he had served God faithfully his whole life and was known as a man after God's own heart,[1] David wanted something else more than God. In his desire for another man's wife, David forgot God and violated not only her body but her heart and her marriage. Then, afraid of the conse-quences—the fallout, being found out—he arranged for the death of Uriah, her husband. I think of his fear-driven blind-ness and understand some of this story better.

I have followed Jesus now for more than ten years. I sing hymns in church, I tell others about his mercy and forgiveness, but I have my own cherished fears, rebellions, obsessions, and wounds. I'm driven to succeed, no matter what it costs. I am estranged from my father, and I want it that way. I run from conflict. I lose myself in self-loathing. Wherever I go, I've got more gods than the one who res-cued me in that country church. I'm beginning to know their names: Approval. Success. Self-made. Each of those things is self-protection, a wall I build and bolster, a declaration that I'm the only one I trust to keep myself safe.

When I first raised my hand toward the church ceiling, when I raced off to Bible study in those early years, then to a Christian college to know more about the God who had rescued me, I expected to be better than this. I studied the books of the Bible, memorized passages of Scripture. I thought my life would chart an upward path, the years bringing me steadily nearer and nearer to God, who would free me from my sins and insecurities as I found my full identity in him.

But all along the way, as Psalm 119 recounts, I wander. I distrust God and trust myself instead. I protect my wounds. I choose other gods. I still do sometimes. Sometimes I go days without opening God's Word on my own, without reminding myself of what is true about him, about myself. I swing between worthlessness and pride. The very week I am writing this, I meet my new pastor and, eager to prove my worth, cannily find a way to recite my résumé to him. Afterward, hearing my own words echo in my ears like acid, I wither in shame.

And then there are the daily choices, when I willfully avoid what I know is good and right. In the apostle Paul's words, "what I want to do I do not do, but what I hate I do."[2] How can God still want me? How can God still want *us*? We are a mess of rebellions and wounds, a collection of harms to ourselves and harms from others, even from the start.

Adam and Eve, barefoot on a mossy carpet in a perfect garden, had everything they needed and wanted. But they trusted a serpent and chose power over dependence, self-rule over relationship. Every shattered piece of our world and our stories and ourselves comes from that choice. Human beings broke the first covenant, and we still experience—and sometimes exacerbate—the fallout.

The Hebrews struggled as well. Although they had no merit of their own, God chose this small, unremarkable tribe of people as his beloved. But the people mostly didn't want him. The Psalms engage with this history in a special cluster, Psalms 104–107, that Gordon Wenham calls the "mini-Pentateuch."[3] These four songs follow the story of God's people from Creation to the Promised Land. Here's how its retelling of the Exodus begins:

> [1] Praise the LORD!
>> Give thanks to the LORD, for he is good!
>> His faithful love endures forever.
> [2] Who can list the glorious miracles of the LORD?
>> Who can ever praise him enough?
> [3] There is joy for those who deal justly with others
>> and always do what is right.
> [4] Remember me, LORD, when you show favor to your people;
>> come near and rescue me.
> [5] Let me share in the prosperity of your chosen ones.[4]

Do we hear the Psalm 1 echo? Joy! Prosperity! But the psalmist is unsparing about what followed. One of the richest, proudest nations on earth was brought to its knees by the power of Yahweh on behalf of his beloved. But his just-redeemed people became apathetic. Even in the wilderness, a place of such need, they forgot his loving beneficence. The psalmist writes that they traded their glorious God for a statue of a bull. Their appetites ran wild. They were jealous of Moses and Aaron. They refused to enter the land God prepared for them. And after they did enter the land, some even sacrificed their children to other gods.[5]

Who can keep God's covenant and stay on the Godward path? Not even God's own chosen people, it seems. Not even King David. And definitely not me. We want so many things more than we want God. The Ten Commandments hold up the mirror: We're after other gods, a pantheon of substitutes we sometimes prefer over our Maker and Father. We want some of our neighbor's riches and real estate and lavish life-style. We want a different spouse. We want success in all we do. And even when we want something good—even the love of a father or mother—when we want it more than we want God, we court trouble, we taste death.

How can we bear the weight of our death-making, our life-taking? How can we even bear our own wounds? We cannot. We run and hide, just as Adam and Eve did after eating from the tree of the knowledge of good and evil. Our human story might have ended there—a short story with a tragic ending. But the story goes on through sixty-six books written over fifteen hundred years, each book unspooling a wondrous trail of grace and restoration. Because God never removes his love from us, his everlasting love. He sees the brokenness of our world, and he comes to rescue. He covers our mistakes, forgives our failures and rebellions. He works healing in the places we have experienced deep harm. And he provides a path back to him, to restored relationship.

Even from the beginning, God made a way. The way is Jesus, who would crush the head of the serpent, the instigator of sin.[6] Jesus, the only one who would keep God's covenant perfectly. Who would be crucified to cover our sins and renew a world irretrievably broken. Who would make the path for us back into unhindered intimacy with God.

How do we turn, bend our hearts and our feet to that mercy path again? David himself will show us. After months of turning his back to God, resolute in his passion for Bathsheba, unrepentant for his murder of Uriah, David finds himself held to account. Nathan the prophet confronts him. David's eyes are opened. He finally sees his crimes through God's eyes. He recognizes his violations of Bathsheba and her husband. The stubborn dam of his silence toward God breaks. In a flood of anguish, he cries out,

Have mercy on me, O God,
according to your steadfast love;
according to your abundant mercy
blot out my transgressions.[7]

David knows there is only one place to flee: He throws himself on God's mercy and his *hesed* love. Do you hear the plea and then the relief? He confesses his rebellion, asks to be purged and washed, for his heart to be cleansed and purified from the inside out. And it's given! He experiences God's forgiveness so deeply and thoroughly that by the end of the psalm, he desires others to experience this restoration as well. Psalm 32, another confession psalm written by David, opens with words we don't expect in confession.

Blessed is the one
  whose transgressions are forgiven,
  whose sins are covered.
Blessed is the one
  whose sin the LORD does not count against them
  and in whose spirit is no deceit.[8]

Blessed! Happy! Joyful are we when our sins are covered, forgiven! The Hebrew word here is the same as the opening of Psalm 1. Even from our darkest sins, we can be restored. Fully.

I know that's hard to believe. Maybe every mistake you've made has been met with punishment. Maybe you've lived in a time and place where mercy and goodness were nowhere to be found. Maybe the weight of the broken world has doubled you over for longer than you can remember.

I understand. I still struggle to fully believe this at times, to believe that we need only speak, only turn, confess—both what we have done and the realities of the wounds we carry— and we are made and found clean, pure, and whole again. But I have experienced this healing again and again. Not because I've uttered magic words. Not because a repentant posture instantaneously transforms me from fearful braggart into pure-hearted worshiper. Only the power and mercy of our God can perform such miracles. Listen!

> For as high as the heavens are above the earth,
> so great is his love for those who fear him;
> as far as the east is from the west,
> so far has he removed our transgressions from us.
> As a father has compassion on his children,
> so the LORD has compassion on those who fear him;
> for he knows how we are formed,
> he remembers that we are dust.[9]

Can you hear the psalmist's language straining under the glorious weight of these truths? When we fall and fail, as we will do again and again, we don't have to punish ourselves. When a broken world and broken people crush our souls, we don't have to hide or run away from God. We can run *to* him. We can hide *in* him. Because he is near, so near. "Even if my father and mother abandon me, the LORD will hold me close," David writes.[10] And there, held in his hands, we find forgiveness. We find sweet reunion with our Father. So we write and speak our sins and all the ways sin has battered us. He listens. He sees and hears us; he lifts our leaden burdens and salves our hurting hearts. And no matter what lies in our past, he restores our joy and leads us purehearted into a future we no longer fear.

■ draw near

We are talking about two kinds of confession in this chapter: the confession of our own damage from the shards of this fractured world and the confession of the ways we participate in the breakage. The confession psalms will give us words for both. After my prideful recitation to my pastor, I turned to Psalms 51 and 32. I wrote my way through those words. David is right. Yes, happy! Blessed! I felt it: full forgiveness before my Father. The emptying of my toxic pride and shame. The utter joy of restoration. Like David, I cannot keep this secret. Come with me and experience this for yourself!

In our practice, we're going to dig into Psalms 51, 32, and 40. Before we do, let's remember our acronym for entering into prayer through the Psalms:

NEARING

- **N**otate (Write out the original psalm by hand, an action that uses both sides of the brain.)
- **E**xpress (Use your voice and body gestures/movements to give full expression to the psalm.)
- **A**mplify (Add your response/circumstance/witness to the psalm.)
- **R**ead (Understand the original psalm in its context, reading different versions if desired.)
- **I**dentify (Personalize the psalm to you and/or to your faith community.)

- **N**ew Testament Fulfillment (Add relevant New Testament verses that augment and fulfill the message of the psalm.)
- **G**ather (Share psalm-prayers in worship with your faith community.)

Let's not be afraid of bringing our brokenness to God. He will meet us there. As Tyler Hartford, a Mennonite pastor to pastors, discovered as he wrote into Psalm 32,

> Writing myself into a psalm and expressing it physically moves me from intellectually assenting to deeply experiencing its emotion and content. Those words become more woven into my conversation with my Heavenly Father. Prophet Jeremiah's cry comes alive: "His word is in my heart like a fire, a fire shut up in my bones. I am weary of holding it in; indeed, I cannot."[11]

We will experience the depth of the shadows and the rescue of God in these ways: **Read, Notate, Amplify, New Testament Fulfillment**, and **Express**.

Read

Read Psalms 51, 32, and 40. All three of these psalms were written by King David, the first two likely in response to his adultery with Bathsheba and murder of Uriah. Psalm 51 gives us the words often sung in worship: "Create in me a clean heart, O God; and renew a right spirit within me."[12]

Psalm 32 appears to be written in response to God's cleansing of his sins. Notice the range of emotions, the gut-level honesty, the almost exuberant sense of relief and joy David feels after he repents. Psalm 40 shifts the focus, allowing us to bring the wounds we carry before our Father, where we experience full rescue and restoration.

Psalm 51 (ESV)

TO THE CHOIRMASTER. A PSALM OF DAVID, WHEN NATHAN THE PROPHET WENT TO HIM, AFTER HE HAD GONE IN TO BATHSHEBA.

¹ Have mercy on me, O God,
   according to your steadfast love;
according to your abundant mercy
   blot out my transgressions.
² Wash me thoroughly from my iniquity,
   and cleanse me from my sin!

³ For I know my transgressions,
   and my sin is ever before me.
⁴ Against you, you only, have I sinned
   and done what is evil in your sight,
so that you may be justified in your words
   and blameless in your judgment.
⁵ Behold, I was brought forth in iniquity,
   and in sin did my mother conceive me.
⁶ Behold, you delight in truth in the inward being,
   and you teach me wisdom in the secret
      heart.

⁷ Purge me with hyssop, and I shall be clean;
 wash me, and I shall be whiter than snow.
⁸ Let me hear joy and gladness;
 let the bones that you have broken rejoice.
⁹ Hide your face from my sins,
 and blot out all my iniquities.
¹⁰ Create in me a clean heart, O God,
 and renew a right spirit within me.
¹¹ Cast me not away from your presence,
 and take not your Holy Spirit from me.
¹² Restore to me the joy of your salvation,
 and uphold me with a willing spirit.

¹³ Then I will teach transgressors your ways,
 and sinners will return to you.
¹⁴ Deliver me from bloodguiltiness, O God,
 O God of my salvation,
 and my tongue will sing aloud of your righteousness.
¹⁵ O Lord, open my lips,
 and my mouth will declare your praise.
¹⁶ For you will not delight in sacrifice, or I would give it;
 you will not be pleased with a burnt offering.
¹⁷ The sacrifices of God are a broken spirit;
 a broken and contrite heart, O God,
 you will not despise.

¹⁸ Do good to Zion in your good pleasure;
 build up the walls of Jerusalem;

[19] then will you delight in right sacrifices,
>> in burnt offerings and whole burnt offerings;
>> then bulls will be offered on your altar.

Psalm 32 (NLT)

A PSALM OF DAVID.

[1] Oh, what joy for those
>> whose disobedience is forgiven,
>> whose sin is put out of sight!

[2] Yes, what joy for those
>> whose record the LORD has cleared of guilt,
>> whose lives are lived in complete honesty!

[3] When I refused to confess my sin,
>> my body wasted away,
>> and I groaned all day long.

[4] Day and night your hand of discipline was heavy on me.
>> My strength evaporated like water in the summer heat.

Interlude

[5] Finally, I confessed all my sins to you
>> and stopped trying to hide my guilt.
I said to myself, "I will confess my rebellion to
>> the LORD."
>> And you forgave me! All my guilt is gone.

Interlude

[6] Therefore, let all the godly pray to you while there is still time,
>> that they may not drown in the floodwaters of judgment.

[7] For you are my hiding place;
    you protect me from trouble.
    You surround me with songs of victory.
Interlude

[8] The LORD says, "I will guide you along the best
    pathway for your life.
    I will advise you and watch over you.
[9] Do not be like a senseless horse or mule
    that needs a bit and bridle to keep it
    under control."

[10] Many sorrows come to the wicked,
    but unfailing love surrounds those who trust the LORD.
[11] So rejoice in the LORD and be glad, all you who obey him!
    Shout for joy, all you whose hearts are pure!

Psalm 40 (NLT)

FOR THE CHOIR DIRECTOR: A PSALM OF DAVID.

[1] I waited patiently for the LORD to help me,
    and he turned to me and heard my cry.
[2] He lifted me out of the pit of despair,
    out of the mud and the mire.
He set my feet on solid ground
    and steadied me as I walked along.
[3] He has given me a new song to sing,
    a hymn of praise to our God.

Many will see what he has done and be amazed.
They will put their trust in the LORD.

4 Oh, the joys of those who trust the LORD,
who have no confidence in the proud
or in those who worship idols.
5 O LORD my God, you have performed many
wonders for us.
Your plans for us are too numerous to list.
You have no equal.
If I tried to recite all your wonderful deeds,
I would never come to the end of them.

6 You take no delight in sacrifices or offerings.
Now that you have made me listen, I finally understand—
you don't require burnt offerings or sin offerings.
7 Then I said, "Look, I have come.
As is written about me in the Scriptures:
8 I take joy in doing your will, my God,
for your instructions are written on my heart."

9 I have told all your people about your justice.
I have not been afraid to speak out,
as you, O LORD, well know.
10 I have not kept the good news of your justice hidden
in my heart;

I have talked about your faithfulness and
saving power.
I have told everyone in the great assembly
of your unfailing love and faithfulness.

[11] LORD, don't hold back your tender mercies
from me.
Let your unfailing love and faithfulness always protect me.
[12] For troubles surround me—
too many to count!
My sins pile up so high
I can't see my way out.
They outnumber the hairs on my head.
I have lost all courage.

[13] Please, LORD, rescue me!
Come quickly, LORD, and help me.
[14] May those who try to destroy me
be humiliated and put to shame.
May those who take delight in my trouble
be turned back in disgrace.
[15] Let them be horrified by their shame,
for they said, "Aha! We've got him now!"

[16] But may all who search for you
be filled with joy and gladness in you.
May those who love your salvation
repeatedly shout, "The LORD is great!"

¹⁷ As for me, since I am poor and needy,
let the LORD keep me in his thoughts.
You are my helper and my savior.
O my God, do not delay.

Notate

1. Choose the psalm that you know you need right now.
   The perceived size or weight of the transgression or pain
   doesn't matter. Any part of the brokenness of the world
   can cause us to distance ourselves from our Father.

2. Write the verses out by hand, thoughtfully. Leave space for
   response either beneath or beside the original words. As
   you go, notice verses that seem to open the door to your
   own expressions.

Amplify

Anywhere in the psalm that you sense an open door, **Amplify**
the verses with your own confession and experience. For
example:

Have mercy on me, O God,
according to your steadfast love;
according to your abundant mercy
blot out my transgressions.
Wash me thoroughly from my
iniquity,
and cleanse me from my sin!

> For I know my transgressions,
> and my sin is ever before me.[13]

> *I have been wrapped up in my own concerns, blind*
> *to so many needs around me. You desire*
> *that we would "love our neighbors."*
> *I have ignored my neighbors' needs,*
> *though I knew them and have the means to help.*
> *Forgive my selfishness!*

Sometimes our confessions are stronger, our transgressions deeper, our wounds seemingly impossible to tend to. It can feel scary to confess these before God, to bring language to attitudes or actions we struggle to face. But God promises to cleanse us. David himself confidently proclaims to us, "Unfailing love surrounds those who trust the LORD!"[14] Trust him and write!

New Testament Fulfillment

The second *N* in our *NEARING* acronym can also help us interact with the confession psalms: adding New Testament passages. Here are some passages that may give us further courage and confidence:

> If we confess our sins, he is faithful and just and will forgive us our sins and purify us from all unrighteousness.[15]

> Godly sorrow brings repentance that leads to salvation and leaves no regret, but worldly sorrow brings death.[16]

The Lord is not slow in keeping his promise, as some understand slowness. Instead he is patient with you, not wanting anyone to perish, but everyone to come to repentance.[17]

Or do you show contempt for the riches of his kindness, forbearance and patience, not realizing that God's kindness is intended to lead you to repentance?[18]

Write out the New Testament promise that connects to what you have already written for your psalm-prayer. For example, Psalm 32:5:

Finally, I confessed all my sins to you
and stopped trying to hide my guilt.
I said to myself, "I will confess my rebellion to the LORD."

You promise that "if we confess our sins, he is faithful and just and will forgive us our sins and purify us from all unrighteousness."
Let me confess my sin now: _____

_____

_____

Express

Lift your words off the page and present them before your Father, who longs to hear them. Here are some suggestions for bringing your whole self before God in this confessional psalm:

- One traditional Jewish movement for confession is to gently touch one's chest with a closed fist as an expression of "I'm sorry" while reading or speaking confessional words.[19]

- Also, bending the head down displays contrition.

- Kneeling is a universal posture of submission and contrition.

- As you reach the verses of celebration of God's goodness and forgiveness, lift your arms, hands open and splayed.

Confession Psalms[20]

Individual

Psalms 6, 15, 32, 51, 58, 88, 123, 130, 143

Communal

Psalms 78, 81, 106

beholding creation

Psalm 8

FOR THE CHOIR DIRECTOR: A PSALM OF DAVID,
TO BE ACCOMPANIED BY A STRINGED INSTRUMENT.

¹O Lord, our Lord, your majestic name fills the earth!
Your glory is higher than the heavens.
²You have taught children and infants
to tell of your strength,
silencing your enemies
and all who oppose you.

³When I look at the night sky and see the work of
your fingers—
the moon and the stars you set in place—
⁴what are mere mortals that you should think
about them,
human beings that you should care for them?
⁵Yet you made them only a little lower than God
and crowned them with glory and honor.

⁶You gave them charge of everything you made,
    putting all things under their authority—
⁷the flocks and the herds
    and all the wild animals,
⁸the birds in the sky, the fish in the sea,
    and everything that swims the ocean
        currents.

⁹O LORD, our Lord, your majestic name fills the earth!

Our years in grad school are done. Shortly after graduation, we make the move: leaving Bear Island and moving to Harvester Island, two miles away. No one has lived here for thirty years. We spend the winter building our house. It's still unfinished, except for parts of the kitchen, our bedroom, and the living room. The front room looks out over a brilliant azure bay and emerald mountains, some still with snow.

We're down on the beach now, our little family: my son, Noah, two and a half; my daughter, Naphtali, four. It's evening, eight thirty, still as bright as noon. A skiff with two figures in neon orange roars past the beach, off to the fishing nets around the island.

"There goes Daddy!" Naphtali calls in her munchkin voice. "When will he be back?"

"He'll be back around midnight, when you're sleeping," I tell her. "But you'll see him in the morning."

As Duncan's skiff disappears around the island, my mind and heart follow him. I know what's ahead for the skiffs tonight. It's take-up night, when arm over arm they pull all the nets out of the water, as directed by Fish and Game. We do this at least a dozen times a summer, often in crisis mode: sometimes when storms rage, or the nets are full of fish or kelp or both. I think of the last time I went out to help. My back remembers. My hands remember, crabbed with carpal tunnel syndrome as I picked fish from the nets as fast as I could.

"Look at the otter!" Noah calls now in his raspy voice, pointing just offshore.

"Ha! He's so fat!" Naphtali laughs. The otter's just a hundred feet away, cruising on the float of his body, noisily cracking a cluster of clams on his chest.

"Do you see that?" I squat beside Noah and point. "He's having clams for lunch!"

The otter doesn't mind our presence at all. Every few seconds he does a full body roll, clasping the shells. Another series of chomps fills the air until the next roll. Every time his whiskered face emerges, we laugh. A pair of oystercatchers bomb past us now, their long orange beaks slicing the air, shrieking as they go.

When I came to these waters and islands, their raw resplendence entranced me—this land and sea sculpted by wind, tidal waters, rain and snow, set on fire by a sun that still flames near midnight. But I did not know that the work of fishing could bend us so low that we might miss it.

I want something different for my children, and maybe it is possible now. We moved from the other island so we could do more than make a living: We want to make a life here. In just a few years, these kids will be joining the men in the skiff, and I worry about that. But we have these years now. I want to make the most of them.

"C'mon, let's go out to the spit," I call. We turn into the wind now and walk out on this graveled peninsula, ocean breaking on both sides, toward the profile of the island.

Living here still feels fresh and new. We don't have running water. Noah sleeps in the woodshop. We bathe once a week in an outhouse that doubles as a wood-fired bathhouse. But none of this matters to me. I wonder if this is how the Hebrews felt as they left Egypt behind and entered the Promised Land. How will we live with God in this spacious new place? I am hopeful, and I am also tired.

Motherhood is both infinitely better and infinitely harder than I imagined. I wake often in the middle of the night, questions stirring my heart. I want so much for my children. I want them to have what I didn't: time to play amid the work. I want them to know they are fully loved. I want them to know the One who made them, that they are fearfully and wonderfully made. I want them to know that God is with them wherever they are. That this whole wild, watery world and everything in it is his.

So we read Bible stories every day, we pray together, we sing, and we go outside. We throw rocks on the beach, climb the deer trails, run through the alder woods, picnic in the meadow, point at shooting stars, and wait for sunsets. I want my kids to hear God's voice in the pages of his book, his remarkable rescue story, and I want them to hear him through the pages of creation.

That's where I first found God as a child: mucking around in the frog pond across the street, marveling at centipedes scuttling beneath the rocks, nursing baby birds, naming the stars from the limbs of maple trees. The creation psalms take us there too, offering a language of prayer somehow both within and beyond words. Among the emotional tumult of lament and confession, suddenly we're given a place to rest and behold. King David, who likely wrote most of the creation psalms, calls us out into the fields, over hills, into the desert, and out under the stars.

Psalm 8, sandwiched between wrenching laments, is the first psalm-prayer of awe to appear in the Psalter. I imagine David, eyes to the heavens, calling out,

LORD, our Lord,
　　how majestic is your name in all the earth!
You have set your glory
　　in the heavens.[1]

In Psalm 19, he does more than gaze at the skies—he listens as the universe, spoken into place, answers back:

The heavens declare the glory of God,
　　and the sky above proclaims his handiwork.
Day to day pours out speech,
　　and night to night reveals knowledge.[2]

How often did the king, governing an entire nation, take time to contemplate the stars? I wonder if his officials raised their eyebrows every time he took off into the hillsides, the mulberry groves. Not only was the king responsible to lead and protect his nation from enemies inside and out, but he was a pastor, too, a shepherd-king charged with guiding his people in love and obedience to Yahweh. Why then does he write songs about the hyrax, the mountain goats, and the stork?[3] If we're to walk with our God along the Psalm 1 path, surely then we're to keep our eyes on God's commands, on his commandments, on the psalms of wisdom, meditating day and night on his Word! Is that not what faithfulness requires?

But David knew the scrolls weren't enough. Because the God who spoke with us, who gave us the wealth of his Word, is also the God who gave us the wonder of his world. He comes near through his Word, and he comes close through his creation. If we don't know and see this, we will miss so much of who he is and how he longs to be with us.

The creation psalms answer the early Israelites' deepest questions—and ours as well. Who is this God we're trying to follow? How powerful is he? What is he like?

The three psalms of the mini-Pentateuch retell Israel's story, beginning with creation. No one witnessed the fireworks of God's world-making words, but in Psalm 104 God himself lifts the veil on the mystery. He inspires the psalmist with breathtaking images of his creative acts: covering, stretching, laying, making, walking in the just-made world. Here's the passage in Young's Literal Translation, which gives us a fuller sense of the vibrancy of the verbs:

> Bless, O my soul, Jehovah! Jehovah, my God,
> Thou hast been very great, Honour and majesty
> Thou hast put on.
> Covering Himself [with] light as a garment,
> Stretching out the heavens as a curtain,
> Who is laying the beam of His upper chambers
> in the waters,
> Who is making thick clouds His chariot,
> Who is walking on wings of wind,
> Making His messengers—the winds,
> His ministers—the flaming fire.[4]

And we are here too, his very own creation. Look how he nourishes us:

> Watering hills from His upper chambers,
> From the fruit of Thy works is the earth satisfied.
> Causing grass to spring up for cattle,
> And herb for the service of man,
> To bring forth bread from the earth,
> And wine—it rejoiceth the heart of man,
> To cause the face to shine from oil,
> And bread—the heart of man it supporteth.[5]

How far does God's creative power reach? All the way from the universe to the uterus. In Psalm 139 we discover we are, each of us, God's own design.

For You formed my inward parts;
    You covered me in my mother's womb.
I will praise You, for I am fearfully and wonderfully made;
    Marvelous are Your works,
    And that my soul knows very well.
My frame was not hidden from You,
    When I was made in secret,
    And skillfully wrought in the lowest parts of the earth.[6]

Again and again the Psalms tell us, "The earth is full of his unfailing love."[7]

All this was news to the early Israelites. In Egypt, God's people heard a different story: that they were disposable, useful only for their work; that the world was created and ruled by thousands of gods, not just one; that these gods were interested in fear and retribution, not love. Even as God was crafting the covenant between himself and his people whom he had rescued, they were creating a golden idol of the Egyptian bull god Apis. They wandered soon after in a desert of their own making, disbelieving who God said he was and who he said they were. Throughout their history, whenever they worshiped Yahweh's creation but rejected Yahweh's presence, they found themselves conquered, unmoored, or exiled to faraway lands.

Now, all these generations later, we are still unmoored,

wandering, so often valuing ourselves and one another by our work. Wherever we work—in corporate buildings, in windowless warehouses, or even out on the ocean—our heads bend low. Our work weeks spill into the weekends. We're trying to pay our bills. We're trying to outrun inflation. We want good schools for our kids. We want our businesses to succeed. In this age of anxiety and insomnia, we miss the witness of the heavens. Our eyes are distracted, and we miss the glory of God. Like the Israelites in the desert, we forget who we are, whose we are. We can find no rest.

We need a rest stop, and here it's given. The creation psalms slow us down. They open our eyes and ears, reminding us of our Creator and our createdness: He is our Father, and he fashioned each of us in our mothers' wombs. We are beloved, given a place of honor among a creation where every inch and acre claps, shouts, sings, whispers, declares the care and the nearness of its Maker. No matter where we live— on an island, in the heart of a city, in a desert valley, in the southern suburbs—drawing near to God means beholding the light of God's Word and of God's world.

So go outside. Walk the beach, watch the birds, wonder at the night's chandeliers overhead. God is lighting those candles every night for us to find our way home.

■ draw near

When we think of creation, our thoughts often go first to the vast created world around us. But creation helps us remember our createdness, our wrestling with the most essential truths about ourselves: *Whose am I? Am I an accident? How did I get here?*

In other cultures' creation stories, the gods displayed world-making power but remained inexplicable, distant, impersonal. Yahweh's creative power, however, is also personal, extending all the way to the shaping and forming of each child in the womb.

In our practice, we're going to dig into Psalm 139, Psalm 8, and Psalm 104. Before we do, let's remember our acronym for entering into prayer through the Psalms:

NEARING

- **N**otate (Write out the original psalm by hand, an action that uses both sides of the brain.)
- **E**xpress (Use your voice and body gestures/movements to give full expression to the psalm.)
- **A**mplify (Add your response/circumstance/witness to the psalm.)
- **R**ead (Understand the original psalm in its context, reading different versions if desired.)
- **I**dentify (Personalize the psalm to you and/or to your faith community.)
- **N**ew Testament Fulfillment (Add relevant New Testament verses that augment and fulfill the message of the psalm.)
- **G**ather (Share psalm-prayers in worship with your faith community.)

The apostle Paul tells us that "we are [God's] work-manship."[8] The Greek word translated here as "workman-ship" is *poiema*, which is related to the English word *poem*. When we are discouraged, under attack, doubting our worth, let David's own poems about us—God's poems—show us who we are. We will enter these words and discover all they have for each of us in these ways: **Express**, **Read**, **Notate**, **Amplify**, and **Identify**.

Express

Psalm 139 lifts the veil on the mystery of our own creation and identity. Because of its importance, it's likely that each of us will turn to this psalm often. We're beginning with **Express** rather than **Notate** because it's vital to understand our createdness in embodied ways.

1. Read the psalm through, aloud if possible. How can we internalize and metabolize these truths about God and his fearful and wonderful work—which is us? Let's activate our bodies and both sides of our brains.

2. As you read the psalm aloud, "*verb*-alize" the passage. Gently connect the action words into a prayer stretch exercise. Here are suggestions to get you started:

   - *searched* (right arm stretching from left to right)
   - *sit* (bend at the knees, back straight as if sitting on a chair)

- *rise* (straighten to standing position)
- *going out, lying down* (intentional heel-to-toe walking, then head resting on shoulder)
- *hem* (draw an imaginary boundary around yourself)
- *lay your hand upon me* (cradle your face with one hand)
- *go from your Spirit* (tip body in a circular motion)
- *flee* (large step to the side and back)
- *go up to the heavens* (stretch as high as you can)
- *make my bed in the depths* (reach lower)
- *rise on the wings of the dawn* (spread arms as you bend at the knees and rise)
- *hold me fast* (hands holding sides of arms, or hugging gesture)

Stop there and feel that last trusting posture, or continue the psalm on your own. You are well on your way to connecting with God in this space beyond language, in the glory of being a created one among his creation.

Psalm 139 (NIV)

FOR THE DIRECTOR OF MUSIC. OF DAVID. A PSALM.

¹You have searched me, LORD,
    and you know me.
²You know when I sit and when I rise;
    you perceive my thoughts from afar.
³You discern my going out and my lying down;
    you are familiar with all my ways.

[4] Before a word is on my tongue
    you, LORD, know it completely.
[5] You hem me in behind and before,
    and you lay your hand upon me.
[6] Such knowledge is too wonderful for me,
    too lofty for me to attain.

[7] Where can I go from your Spirit?
    Where can I flee from your presence?
[8] If I go up to the heavens, you are there;
    if I make my bed in the depths, you are there.
[9] If I rise on the wings of the dawn,
    if I settle on the far side of the sea,
[10] even there your hand will guide me,
    your right hand will hold me fast.
[11] If I say, "Surely the darkness will hide me
    and the light become night around me,"
[12] even the darkness will not be dark to you;
    the night will shine like the day,
    for darkness is as light to you.

[13] For you created my inmost being;
    you knit me together in my mother's womb.
[14] I praise you because I am fearfully and wonderfully made;
    your works are wonderful,
    I know that full well.
[15] My frame was not hidden from you
    when I was made in the secret place,

when I was woven together in the depths
of the earth.

[16] Your eyes saw my unformed body;
all the days ordained for me were written in
your book
before one of them came to be.

[17] How precious to me are your thoughts, God!
How vast is the sum of them!

[18] Were I to count them,
they would outnumber the grains of sand—
when I awake, I am still with you.

[19] If only you, God, would slay the wicked!
Away from me, you who are bloodthirsty!

[20] They speak of you with evil intent;
your adversaries misuse your name.

[21] Do I not hate those who hate you, LORD,
and abhor those who are in rebellion
against you?

[22] I have nothing but hatred for them;
I count them my enemies.

[23] Search me, God, and know my heart;
test me and know my anxious thoughts.

[24] See if there is any offensive way in me,
and lead me in the way everlasting.

When Naomi, one of my psalm students, spent time in this
psalm, she experienced a breakthrough:

The issues of heart I have been facing involve believing Satan's lies, illusions, and fantasies of who I am—my identity. But as I have pursued God through Psalm 139, he has met me. God has graciously given me revelation of my clean standing in him, and when my heart struggled to be able to accept even that, God graciously broke down the prison door, shattered the chains holding me, blew apart the lies, the fortress, the stronghold, and set me *free.*[9]

Read, Notate, and Amplify

Psalm 8 is another psalm of David. This one is short, just nine verses, but in these powerful poetic lines we return to Genesis and discover who we are and why we are here. Notice how the verses move us positionally from "higher than the heavens" all the way down to under the sea, creating a sense of completion. This sweep of creation is then contained within the frame of God's glory and the majesty of his name, which begin and end the psalm.

But there's something unusual in these verses. Do you hear the incredulity in David's voice at this paradox? How can it be that we, mere earthen, mortal creatures, should be given so much honor and glory? How can it be that we've received this unique role of authority over God's entire created order, a role that has not changed despite our modern, often urban, lives? There's no answer given in the psalm, except that this is the goodness and gift of God. We have this opportunity now to slow down and to consider the remarkable position

God has given us as caretakers of a world he created, blessed, named "very good,"[10] and then placed within our hands.

Psalm 8 (NLT)

FOR THE CHOIR DIRECTOR: A PSALM OF DAVID, TO BE ACCOMPANIED BY A STRINGED INSTRUMENT.

1 O LORD, our Lord, your majestic name fills the earth!
Your glory is higher than the heavens.
2 You have taught children and infants
to tell of your strength,
silencing your enemies
and all who oppose you.

3 When I look at the night sky and see the work of your
fingers—
the moon and the stars you set in place—
4 what are mere mortals that you should think
about them,
human beings that you should care for them?
5 Yet you made them only a little lower than God
and crowned them with glory and honor.
6 You gave them charge of everything you made,
putting all things under their authority—
7 the flocks and the herds
and all the wild animals,
8 the birds in the sky, the fish in the sea,
and everything that swims the ocean currents.

9 O LORD, our Lord, your majestic name fills the earth!

1. **Read** through the psalm, and then **Notate** the psalm; write it out by hand, leaving space beneath each verse.

2. **Amplify** each verse by responding in your own words as you feel led.

Identify

In Psalm 104, the psalmist offers a stunning poetic retelling of the creation story in Genesis. We see God speaking, thundering, rebuking, feeding, watering—authoring with his thundering and tender words the complete cosmos, from the heavens to the soil, from plants to creatures—all this a means of seeing, hearing, and knowing the heart of our Creator.

To engage Psalm 104, you'll **Identify** God's creativity and creation around you, wherever you live. If you're able, bring this book and a notebook, and go out on a walk or a drive to a favorite spot. We're so much more than our minds: We've been given bodies and brains intricately wired to apprehend and enjoy God's lavish world. Let's use the gifts we've been given!

Psalm 104 (ESV)

¹Bless the LORD, O my soul!
   O LORD my God, you are very great!
   You are clothed with splendor and majesty,
²covering yourself with light as with a garment,
   stretching out the heavens like a tent.

³ He lays the beams of his chambers on the waters;
    he makes the clouds his chariot;
    he rides on the wings of the wind;
⁴ he makes his messengers winds,
    his ministers a flaming fire.

⁵ He set the earth on its foundations,
    so that it should never be moved.
⁶ You covered it with the deep as with a garment;
    the waters stood above the mountains.
⁷ At your rebuke they fled;
    at the sound of your thunder they took to flight.
⁸ The mountains rose, the valleys sank down
    to the place that you appointed for them.
⁹ You set a boundary that they may not pass,
    so that they might not again cover the earth.

¹⁰ You make springs gush forth in the valleys;
    they flow between the hills;
¹¹ they give drink to every beast of the field;
    the wild donkeys quench their thirst.
¹² Beside them the birds of the heavens dwell;
    they sing among the branches.
¹³ From your lofty abode you water the mountains;
    the earth is satisfied with the fruit of your work.

¹⁴ You cause the grass to grow for the livestock
    and plants for man to cultivate,

that he may bring forth food from the earth
¹⁵ and wine to gladden the heart of man,
oil to make his face shine
and bread to strengthen man's heart.
¹⁶ The trees of the LORD are watered abundantly,
the cedars of Lebanon that he planted.
¹⁷ In them the birds build their nests;
the stork has her home in the fir trees.
¹⁸ The high mountains are for the wild goats;
the rocks are a refuge for the rock badgers.

¹⁹ He made the moon to mark the seasons;
the sun knows its time for setting.
²⁰ You make darkness, and it is night,
when all the beasts of the forest creep
about.
²¹ The young lions roar for their prey,
seeking their food from God.
²² When the sun rises, they steal away
and lie down in their dens.
²³ Man goes out to his work
and to his labor until the evening.

²⁴ O LORD, how manifold are your works!
In wisdom have you made them all;
the earth is full of your creatures.
²⁵ Here is the sea, great and wide,
which teems with creatures innumerable,

living things both small and great.
²⁶ There go the ships,
and Leviathan, which you formed to play in it.

²⁷ These all look to you,
to give them their food in due season.
²⁸ When you give it to them, they gather it up;
when you open your hand, they are filled with
good things.
²⁹ When you hide your face, they are dismayed;
when you take away their breath, they die
and return to their dust.
³⁰ When you send forth your Spirit, they are created,
and you renew the face of the ground.

³¹ May the glory of the LORD endure forever;
may the LORD rejoice in his works,
³² who looks on the earth and it trembles,
who touches the mountains and they smoke!
³³ I will sing to the LORD as long as I live;
I will sing praise to my God while I have being.
³⁴ May my meditation be pleasing to him,
for I rejoice in the LORD.
³⁵ Let sinners be consumed from the earth,
and let the wicked be no more!
Bless the LORD, O my soul!
Praise the LORD!

1. As you arrive at your chosen spot, take a few minutes to quiet yourself and enter into whatever creation scene surrounds you. Breathe deeply. Feel the fresh air on your face. Listen for birds, the sounds of water, leaves muttering in the breeze. Watch snow swirling and settling. Notice flowers bending and straightening. Feel the connection as a fellow participant in God's magnificent creation, knowing and trusting that sense of belonging.

2. To **Identify** in your own psalm-prayer, you can follow the pattern of Psalm 104 or take a more free-form approach. Simply describe in either prose or poetry what you see of God's hand and character in the weather, in the flora and fauna of your neighborhood and surroundings. Be as specific as possible! Let these questions guide and evoke your observations and interactions:

- If there is a body of water nearby, describe the water. How does it move and change?
- What do you see of God in its movement and activity?
- What animals do you often see in this place?
- What do these animals look like, sound like?
- How does God take care of them?
- What do you learn about God from these creatures?
- What trees and notable flowers and plants are around you?
- What do you see through them about God's care?

Creation Psalms[11]

The theme of creation is found throughout the Psalms, but these psalms focus primarily on God's original act of creation and his ongoing care within creation.

Psalms 8, 19, 29, 104, 139, 148

chapter seven

rejoicing in thanksgiving

Psalm 138 (HCSB)
A THANKFUL HEART

DAVIDIC.

¹ I will give You thanks with all my heart;
     I will sing Your praise before the heavenly
          beings.
² I will bow down toward Your holy temple
     and give thanks to Your name
     for Your constant love and truth.
You have exalted Your name
     and Your promise above everything else.
³ On the day I called, You answered me;
     You increased strength within me.

⁴ All the kings on earth will give You thanks, LORD,
     when they hear what You have promised.
⁵ They will sing of the LORD's ways,
     for the LORD's glory is great.

⁶Though the LORD is exalted,
   He takes note of the humble;
   but He knows the haughty from
      a distance.

⁷If I walk into the thick of danger,
   You will preserve my life
   from the anger of my enemies.
You will extend Your hand;
   Your right hand will save me.
⁸The LORD will fulfill His purpose for me.
   LORD, Your love is eternal;
   do not abandon the work of Your hands.

It's the morning of Thanksgiving. We're going over to my sister- and brother-in-law's. The kids are all excited, but I'm not sure I have the strength to go. Our new son, Micah, is nestled beside me in bed.

He was born three days ago—on my forty-fifth birthday. Duncan threw me a party in the hospital a few hours after the birth, with twenty family members and friends and a cake made by a French pastry chef. "I'm so proud of you," he said. "And I want you to know that your birthday will always be special." I could have cried right there in my hospital bed, chocolate cake in my mouth.

We are learning again to relinquish, to surrender to this God, the maker of life. This Father who, two years before, decided that four fierce, beautiful kids were not enough.

That we needed another son, who would be followed by yet another who would share my birthday. Where will this pilgrim path wind and thread? What lumpy fields will it traverse, what valleys will it descend, what mountains will it cross? I have a lot of complaints right now about what feel like rocky detours. Another year of nursing through short nights, returning to diapers, giving up teaching, in midlife starting over—again. Do I really have the endurance to raise teen boys into my midsixties? Surely I sound as grumbly and whiny to God as the Hebrews did while complaining about their bread from heaven.

At the Thanksgiving table, exhausted, I know I should be thankful. God has delivered me and this baby safely through the pregnancy, and he is perfect. But my heart fills with fatigue and worry for the years ahead. I don't know what to do except to return to the central message of the Psalms: Yahweh reigns. Every day of the pregnancies and every day with these little ones are filled with exhaustion, lament, nursery rhymes, wonder, confession. I lay my hands open before God. These babies grow.

Micah is six months old now. Abraham is two and a half. We're leaving for Harvester Island in two days. I have made this migration now for twenty-five seasons. I am trying to gather food, books, toys, diapers—all the accoutrements needed for six kids on a wilderness island for three months. I am trying not to panic. After the fourth child I gave away all our baby things, and local flea markets and thrift stores have filled in the gaps since. Every gap except one. One small thing that I would almost trade everything else for—a baby backpack. For my first four babies, I had a blue Kelty backpack, the only one I found that fit my long-legged, short-waisted body.

Hiking is my sanity on a rainy, roadless island where there is nowhere to go except two small trails. We feel like pioneers on those trails, crashing through the underbrush, watching the eagles, surprising deer, eating buckets of berries. Now, with two more little ones, I can't take them on the trails without a backpack. They cost too much to buy new. I've been stopping at the Salvation Army in Kodiak several times this month, checking, hoping, but now, two days before my gang and I scramble into the bush plane, it's too late. The prospect of a summer on the island without a backpack nearly smothers me.

This day, I am driving back from the grocery store with last-minute provisions. The Salvation Army is just a half mile from here. I decide to stop one last time before I go.

I am so harried with preparations that I do not pray, unless tiny little wish-making thoughts count. I don't want to treat God like Santa Claus, like a vending machine that exists to satisfy my every whim. Terrible things are happening in the world. How can this matter?

I open the door and walk in, past a table with Bibles, hoping maybe I can at least snag a baby sweatshirt or an extra pair of shoes for Abraham. A red-haired woman behind the counter glances up and greets me: "Hi! How are you?" My eyes are already casting over the racks of tired clothes, the shelves of books, the kitchen bric-a-brac lining the walls.

"Good. I'm looking for a baby backpack."

"Oh! We just got one an hour ago. It's in the back with the baby stuff."

I catch my breath. Stay calm. In eight steps I am picking up a blue Kelty backpack, the exact model I gave away a few years ago. This one is nicer. It's nearly new. It's five dollars. I blink back tears as I pull out the money and hand it to her.

I am not David fighting a battle against a nation that wants to destroy Israel. I am not being pursued by an army trying to kill me. I am not dying of a sickness. I am not facing bankruptcy or the loss of my home or a loved one. The psalmists and many others throughout history, and many others around me, know these depths. But in these years of my life I am just a worn-out mother with six children, about to go to a lonely island where everything is given to fishing. And my Father heard me. I could not ask my father or mother for anything, but somehow a God who created billions of people, who is spinning countless galaxies in the infinitude of space, hears my silent fears and sends the exact backpack I need to the Salvation Army in Kodiak just before the last time I look. How can this God bend so low and come so near?

The next days are intense—with packing, a bush-plane trip, a skiff ride—but the gates of my heart have been opened. All that week on the island, I sing under my breath the words we sing nearly every week in church, inspired by Psalm 100: "I will enter his gates with thanksgiving in my heart." I want to live like this always, deeply connected to my Father, filled with gratitude, knowing I am loved.

But the summer goes on, with all its isolations and challenges, and my eyes shift downward. I turn to worry. I turn to fear again. As I do, I feel the return of loneliness, a sense of abandonment. It has happened enough now, though, that I am recognizing this pattern. When I see only what I lack, forget all that's been lavished, God fades away until he feels as distant as the mountains on our horizon.

I believe this happens for many of us.

How do we stay awake and alive to the presence of God and all he is doing in our lives? The psalmists know, and they show us. While we might feel a natural affinity for lament, the Psalter contains twice as many thanksgiving and praise psalms as lament psalms. Thanksgiving psalms will open our eyes to find God no matter how far away he might feel.

Psalm 9 is the first thanksgiving psalm we find in the Psalter. David is thanking God for rescuing him from his enemies.

At least fifty psalms recount God's rescues—rescues from enemies, from abandonment, from illness, from bondage, from storms, from despair. Don't we know this as well? Danger looms and lurks around all of us on the pilgrim path, but we have a God to whom we can cry. He answers, and so many times he delivers.

Psalm 107 recounts four dramatic rescue stories:

> Give thanks to the LORD, for he is good;
> his love endures forever.
> Let the redeemed of the LORD tell their story—
> those he redeemed from the hand of the foe.[1]

At the end of each story, David calls the rescued to "give thanks to the LORD for his unfailing love and his wonderful deeds for mankind."[2]

In other psalms, the writer begins in lament, then writes his way to thanksgiving and praise. In Psalm 28, David cries out to God to hear and deliver him—and near the end of the psalm he knows God has heard his cry:

> Blessed be the LORD!
> For he has heard the voice of my pleas for mercy. . . .
> And with my song I give thanks to him.[3]

Some of the prayer-songs begin immediately with a gush of gratitude for something the Lord has done. Psalm 116 opens,

> I love the LORD, for he heard my voice;
> he heard my cry for mercy.
> Because he turned his ear to me,
> I will call on him as long as I live.[4]

But for most of us, thanksgiving is not our native tongue, not our heart's natural bent. The Hebrews had the same struggle. As we follow their story in the Torah—their rescue from Pharaoh, the Exodus, and the wanderings in the desert, all the way to the entrance into the Promised Land—we don't hear many words of gratitude. They walked in daily miracles: food, water, guidance, protection, sandals that never wore out, bread that fell from heaven, dramatic deliverance from enemies. These provisions were God's gifts to his children, displays of his care, his kindness, his generosity, his love. But the Hebrews didn't see his loving heart. They saw only the darkness and fear in their own. God's gifts were met, then, with suspicion, disbelief, accusation, defiance. The covenant relationship of love God made with his just-redeemed people was violated again and again. Some of those times, death and judgment ensued.

But the Second Torah, the Psalms, recounts the same journey to a very different soundtrack. One-third to one-half of the prayer-songs of God's people, even the psalms that recount the Israelites' painful story, now ring with verses and shouts of thanksgiving to God. How did this happen? How did the same historical events lead to such a different outcome? It's not just revisionist history or a simple language shift. David and the psalmists wrote songs and prayers to lead their people in a heart and vision shift: from the myopia of self-focused grumbling to God-focused gratitude.

We need this shift as much now as the Hebrews needed it then. We seem to be born, most of us, with a negativity bias, but we have additional burdens now. In our time, the news is mostly tragic, loud, ruled by media and social media. Our cultural soundscape has become a cacophony of anger, outrage, and complaint. At the same time, we're urged to pursue our own happiness, yet we're always falling short. Discontent abounds. To quiet the hounds of want for a moment, we keep one day a year to give thanks. We try to redress a year of ingratitude around a feast we worry will get cold if we speak too long, but often our hearts and our eyes change little.

Like the Israelites in the wilderness, we forget to look up, to see beyond ourselves. We're so focused on the future, on growth and progress, that we forget to look behind us. We're so focused on our desires that we can't see what we've already been given.

As David recounts the history of his people, he observes again and again that the people "forgot." When God first brought them into the land, he cautioned them:

Only be on your guard and diligently watch yourselves, so that you don't forget the things your eyes have seen and so that they don't slip from your mind as long as you live. Teach them to your children and your grandchildren.[5]

David, Asaph, and others wrote psalms to help them remember. In those psalms, they recounted their people's travels and travails, but these songs do more than merely recount what happened.

As God's people sing the wrenching stories of their

ancestors' struggles and rebellions, all the original accusations and complaints turn to gratitude and thanksgiving. Because they look up. They remember. Finally, they see: The true gift is not the rescues, the daily provisions, even the miracles. The greatest gift is the love of their compassionate Father. How can they not respond?

David urges them to sing of God's deeds, to tell others, and to bring thank offerings:

> Let them give thanks to the LORD for his
>   unfailing love
> and his wonderful deeds for mankind.
> Let them sacrifice thank offerings
> and tell of his works with songs of joy.[6]

What a time of celebration it was! Unlike the other sacrifices and feasts that God instituted at Mount Sinai, the thank offering was entirely voluntary. When someone received a special gift, rescue, or mercy from the Lord and wanted to thank him publicly, she would bring wine, a double portion of bread, and an animal from her flock. She would gather her family and friends for a large festal meal, large because all the food had to be consumed in one day. Can you see it? The families collected, the friends, the chatter, the laughter, the roasted meat and bread passed 'round and 'round, the gatherer standing before everyone telling "of his works with songs of joy"?

It was not joyous merely because of the presence of family

and friends. God was there too. The whole of it was a beautiful exchange.

In providing gifts for his people and in receiving back their offerings of meat and words of thanks and praise, the Father and his children were present to one another, bound in a whole-bodied, full-hearted relationship of trust and love. In Egypt and other pagan nations, animal sacrifices were made to their gods out of fear of retribution. In contrast, God's people brought sacrifices of thanks and ate before their Father with gratitude and joy. They ate in the presence of God.

Today we have a yet greater reason to gather, speak, and sing our thanks to God and one another. We have been brought even closer to our Father. The thanksgiving sacrifice prefigured the final sacrifice—Christ, the Lamb of God, who died for us so that "now in Christ Jesus you who once were far away have been brought near by the blood of Christ."[7] There is no greater gift. And so we gather in our churches to celebrate the Eucharist. The bread we break is the body of Jesus, broken for us; the wine we drink is his blood, spilled for us. We eat and drink joyfully as people swept from the faraway land of darkness into his right-here-and-now Kingdom of light. We eat and drink knowing our God dwells no longer in the Temple but here within the temple of our bodies. He cannot come any nearer.

But we are human, and sometimes we forget. Especially when our paths and our days twist and sink: the morning I held the pregnancy-test stick in my hand and dropped to the floor; the day I left the island intending never to go back; the nights of mourning my father and mother; the days of wrestling with scrappy sons.

But look! A God whom I sometimes forget does not move away. Even when I'm unable to ask, my Father still comes with his everlasting love, bringing salvation, bearing gifts: a relationship healed. A quiet afternoon. An open door and a hug. Forgiveness for my father. A new son. Six beautiful children. A backpack. Jesus. His never-ending *hesed* love.

We may not always start with thanksgiving, but when we slow down, lift our eyes, see the heart of the giver, we can always end there.

■ draw near

The psalms offer many entry points to gratitude. No matter where we find ourselves, entering and writing into and out of the thanksgiving psalms will not only open our eyes to all God has done and is doing, but it will also create a record of immeasurable worth. One of my favorite activities is to go back through the psalm-prayers I've written over the last two decades, many of them psalms of rescue and gratitude. As I read those words and the circumstances and answers to prayer that engendered them, I am brought to humble thanks before my Father again and again. Let's begin your journal of thanksgiving!

In our practice, we're going to dig into Psalm 107,

Psalm 116, and Psalm 28. Before we do, let's remember our acronym for entering into prayer through the Psalms:

NEARING

- **N**otate (Write out the original psalm by hand, an action that uses both sides of the brain.)
- **E**xpress (Use your voice and body gestures/movements to give full expression to the psalm.)
- **A**mplify (Add your response/circumstance/witness to the psalm.)
- **R**ead (Understand the original psalm in its context, reading different versions if desired.)
- **I**dentify (Personalize the psalm to you and/or to your faith community.)
- **N**ew Testament Fulfillment (Add relevant New Testament verses that augment and fulfill the message of the psalm.)
- **G**ather (Share psalm-prayers in worship with your faith community.)

We will enter these words and discover all they have for each of us in these ways: **Read**, **Notate**, **Identify**, **Amplify**, **Express**, and **Gather**.

Read

Psalm 107 is a remarkable psalm of thanksgiving. In vivid, moving poetry, it unfolds the stories of four rescues of people brought "from east and west, from north and south."[8] It looks backward, through history, but also prefigures the gathering of all the redeemed in Revelation, who are brought to Yahweh's heavenly throne from the four corners of the world, from every tribe and every tongue.[9] Each rescue story ends with a stirring call to give thanks.

Read the psalm through, ideally out loud, paying attention to the vivid images and forceful verbs. Do you find yourself in one of these rescued groups?

Psalm 107 (NIV)

[1] Give thanks to the LORD, for he is good;
   his love endures forever.

[2] Let the redeemed of the LORD tell their story—
   those he redeemed from the hand of the foe,
[3] those he gathered from the lands,
   from east and west, from north and south.

[4] Some wandered in desert wastelands,
   finding no way to a city where they could settle.
[5] They were hungry and thirsty,
   and their lives ebbed away.
[6] Then they cried out to the LORD in their trouble,
   and he delivered them from their distress.
[7] He led them by a straight way
   to a city where they could settle.
[8] Let them give thanks to the LORD for his
      unfailing love
   and his wonderful deeds for mankind,

⁹ for he satisfies the thirsty
   and fills the hungry with good things.

¹⁰ Some sat in darkness, in utter darkness,
   prisoners suffering in iron chains,
¹¹ because they rebelled against God's commands
   and despised the plans of the Most High.
¹² So he subjected them to bitter labor;
   they stumbled, and there was no one to help.
¹³ Then they cried to the LORD in their trouble,
   and he saved them from their distress.
¹⁴ He brought them out of darkness, the utter darkness,
   and broke away their chains.
¹⁵ Let them give thanks to the LORD for his
      unfailing love
   and his wonderful deeds for mankind,
¹⁶ for he breaks down gates of bronze
   and cuts through bars of iron.

¹⁷ Some became fools through their rebellious ways
   and suffered affliction because of their iniquities.
¹⁸ They loathed all food
   and drew near the gates of death.
¹⁹ Then they cried to the LORD in their trouble,
   and he saved them from their distress.
²⁰ He sent out his word and healed them;
   he rescued them from the grave.

²¹ Let them give thanks to the LORD for his
        unfailing love
    and his wonderful deeds for mankind.
²² Let them sacrifice thank offerings
    and tell of his works with songs of joy.

²³ Some went out on the sea in ships;
    they were merchants on the mighty waters.
²⁴ They saw the works of the LORD,
    his wonderful deeds in the deep.
²⁵ For he spoke and stirred up a tempest
    that lifted high the waves.
²⁶ They mounted up to the heavens and went down
        to the depths;
    in their peril their courage melted away.
²⁷ They reeled and staggered like drunkards;
    they were at their wits' end.
²⁸ Then they cried out to the LORD in their trouble,
    and he brought them out of their distress.
²⁹ He stilled the storm to a whisper;
    the waves of the sea were hushed.
³⁰ They were glad when it grew calm,
    and he guided them to their desired haven.
³¹ Let them give thanks to the LORD for his
        unfailing love
    and his wonderful deeds for mankind.
³² Let them exalt him in the assembly of the people
    and praise him in the council of the elders.

[33] He turned rivers into a desert,
    flowing springs into thirsty ground,
[34] and fruitful land into a salt waste,
    because of the wickedness of those who lived there.
[35] He turned the desert into pools of water
    and the parched ground into flowing springs;
[36] there he brought the hungry to live,
    and they founded a city where they could settle.
[37] They sowed fields and planted vineyards
    that yielded a fruitful harvest;
[38] he blessed them, and their numbers greatly increased,
    and he did not let their herds diminish.

[39] Then their numbers decreased, and they were humbled
    by oppression, calamity and sorrow;
[40] he who pours contempt on nobles
    made them wander in a trackless waste.
[41] But he lifted the needy out of their affliction
    and increased their families like flocks.
[42] The upright see and rejoice,
    but all the wicked shut their mouths.

[43] Let the one who is wise heed these things
    and ponder the loving deeds of the LORD.

Notate

Notate the psalm, writing it by hand and leaving space beneath each line for the next part of the practice.

Identify and Amplify

Psalm 107:2 tells us, "Let the redeemed of the LORD tell their story" (NIV). What story has God given you to tell? Using these inspired words, choose one or more stories about God's rescue in your life. **Identify** with the language of the psalm, and then **Amplify** your psalm-prayer with your own experience. Be sure to follow the pattern of this psalm, framing it as the psalmist does:

1. Begin with verses 1-3, giving thanks.

2. Describe the rescue.

3. End with verses 33-43, summarizing God's saving deeds of the past and ongoing deeds in the present.

You can choose to write about your experiences in more metaphorical terms, but if possible, recount specific places and details. As you do, you'll notice consistent themes that will aid in remembering, recording, and paying tribute to God's loving deeds.

In doing this, we enter and experience the rescue story of God's first people, as we should, for their story has become ours. But the story is not over! Because God is alive and present, and his *hesed* love never fails. God is still rescuing his people.

Express and Gather

1. When you're finished, as always, **Express** your words aloud. Consider adding postures or gestures to your

words as you speak them to your Father. The traditional gesture of *todah* is the extension of hands in adoration and acceptance. Pray your psalm to God in that posture, being bodily aware of both the received blessing and the offered thanks. Your extended hands might also become a cup of holding and giving.

2. Consider sharing your psalm or the story behind your psalm publicly: **Gather** with your family and friends, with your faith community. (Why not call a potluck while you're at it?) Most of the psalms of thanksgiving and praise include this crucial element: making God's goodness known to others.

What do we do when we present a need to God and he answers that prayer? Whether the need was large or small, sometimes, in the crush of our lives, we may forget to thank him. Or we simply cast a thank-you heavenward and call it good. David and the other psalmists regard answered prayer as a holy moment we ought to record, respond to, and make known. Rather than simply receiving and even hoarding the gift of the answered need, the psalmists show us how to live a life of out-loud and ongoing thanksgiving.

Notate and Express

Psalm 116 (NIV)
¹I love the LORD, for he heard my voice;
    he heard my cry for mercy.

² Because he turned his ear to me,
    I will call on him as long as I live.

³ The cords of death entangled me,
    the anguish of the grave came over me;
    I was overcome by distress and sorrow.
⁴ Then I called on the name of the LORD:
    "LORD, save me!"

⁵ The LORD is gracious and righteous;
    our God is full of compassion.
⁶ The LORD protects the unwary;
    when I was brought low, he saved me.

⁷ Return to your rest, my soul,
    for the LORD has been good to you.

⁸ For you, LORD, have delivered me from death,
    my eyes from tears,
    my feet from stumbling,
⁹ that I may walk before the LORD
    in the land of the living.

¹⁰ I trusted in the LORD when I said,
    "I am greatly afflicted";
¹¹ in my alarm I said,
    "Everyone is a liar."

¹² What shall I return to the LORD
    for all his goodness to me?

¹³ I will lift up the cup of salvation
    and call on the name of the LORD.
¹⁴ I will fulfill my vows to the LORD
    in the presence of all his people.

¹⁵ Precious in the sight of the LORD
    is the death of his faithful servants.
¹⁶ Truly I am your servant, LORD;
    I serve you just as my mother did;
    you have freed me from my chains.

¹⁷ I will sacrifice a thank offering to you
    and call on the name of the LORD.
¹⁸ I will fulfill my vows to the LORD
    in the presence of all his people,
¹⁹ in the courts of the house of the LORD—
    in your midst, Jerusalem.

    Praise the LORD.

1. **Notate** the psalm, writing it out by hand. Or if time is lim-
    ited, you may want to write your psalm directly with your
    Amplifications, adding your particular circumstances
    and answers to prayer.

2. **Express** your psalm as you speak it before the Lord, and perhaps even before others. These psalms of thanksgiving contain shifts of mood, from despair and death to release and gratitude. As you prepare to read and embody your words, try creating a gesture or posture for each one of these circumstances and shifts. As you **Express** your words, the movement of your body will create a whole-bodied, whole-brained heightening and deepening of your expression of gratitude to the Lord.

Read and Express

We can arrive at thanksgiving through lament as well. As you **Read** Psalm 28, notice how David begins calling out for God's mercy and rescue. Through the first five verses, he delineates his dilemma: He needs deliverance from the wicked. Then in verse six there's a sudden turn, ending the psalm in complete trust and thanks. Composing this psalm of thanksgiving changed his reality and his heart. And it can change yours as well.

Psalm 28 (ESV)
OF DAVID.

¹ To you, O Lord, I call;
    my rock, be not deaf to me,
lest, if you be silent to me,
    I become like those who go down to the pit.
² Hear the voice of my pleas for mercy,
    when I cry to you for help,

when I lift up my hands
 toward your most holy sanctuary.

³ Do not drag me off with the wicked,
 with the workers of evil,
who speak peace with their neighbors
 while evil is in their hearts.
⁴ Give to them according to their work
 and according to the evil of their deeds;
give to them according to the work of their hands;
 render them their due reward.
⁵ Because they do not regard the works of
  the LORD
 or the work of his hands,
 he will tear them down and build them up
  no more.

⁶ Blessed be the LORD!
 For he has heard the voice of my pleas
  for mercy.
⁷ The LORD is my strength and my shield;
 in him my heart trusts, and I am helped;
my heart exults,
 and with my song I give thanks to him.
⁸ The LORD is the strength of his people;
 he is the saving refuge of his anointed.
⁹ Oh, save your people and bless your heritage!
 Be their shepherd and carry them forever.

For this psalm, let's do something different. You are free, always, to **Notate**, to write out each psalm by hand. The time and physical effort invested are always well spent. This time, though, let's present these words aloud just as they are, but we'll **Express** by adding some postures. One person may read the psalm aloud while you or a group respond together bodily. Or you may both **Read** and **Express** the words through these positions.

1. Begin the psalm contracted inward, with arms and hands clenched tightly to the chest, head down.

2. Verse 2: Slowly move from closed to opening wide and upward.

3. End in an organic stance of strength, trust, and tenderness.

Thanksgiving Psalms[10]

Individual

Psalms 9, 18, 28, 30, 32, 34, 40 (verses 2-12), 41, 66 (verses 1-7), 92, 100, 107, 116, 118, 138

Communal

Psalms 66 (verses 8-12), 67, 124, 129

offering praise

Psalm 148

¹ Praise the LORD!

Praise the LORD from the heavens!
> Praise him from the skies!
² Praise him, all his angels!
> Praise him, all the armies of heaven!
³ Praise him, sun and moon!
> Praise him, all you twinkling stars!
⁴ Praise him, skies above!
> Praise him, vapors high above the clouds!
⁵ Let every created thing give praise to
> the LORD,
> for he issued his command, and
> they came into being.
⁶ He set them in place forever and ever.
> His decree will never be revoked.

⁷ Praise the LORD from the earth,
   you creatures of the ocean depths,
⁸ fire and hail, snow and clouds,
   wind and weather that obey him,
⁹ mountains and all hills,
   fruit trees and all cedars,
¹⁰ wild animals and all livestock,
   small scurrying animals and birds,
¹¹ kings of the earth and all people,
   rulers and judges of the earth,
¹² young men and young women,
   old men and children.

¹³ Let them all praise the name of the LORD.
   For his name is very great;
   his glory towers over the earth and heaven!
¹⁴ He has made his people strong,
   honoring his faithful ones—
   the people of Israel who are close to him.

Praise the LORD!

We're on a walk out to Spruce Cape in Kodiak. It's winter, almost Christmas. The ground is frozen, but there is no snow. The spruce trees tower over us, swaying in the wind. I hang back to follow the bundled figures ahead of me. All six of my kids have returned to Alaska with their spouses and children for the holidays. We're a mob. The wind carries laughter and chatter back to me. I've walked this trail so many times over the last thirty years, often with a baby in a backpack, with toddlers and bigger kids running ahead. I can almost hear and see the stories, the stumbles, the races, the stick fights, the songs. Now these children have children.

The trail begins through a metal gate, then gently turns and rises through the shadows of the forest before opening out to the cape. The spruce trees shelter us for the first half, but when we break into the open, onto the field of the cape, the full force of the fifty-mile-per-hour wind hits us. We can hardly stand. We cannot hear one another over the howl. The ocean explodes against the cliffs in roars of foam; the rocks on the beach tumble and rattle under the rollers. Two of my sons spread their arms and lean into the wind, and it holds them. I raise my arms and let the wind wave them wildly. Everything that can move is moving. Everything that can make a sound is speaking.

In a few days we will celebrate the God who started this whole gushing, pulsing world with a sentence, then came among us as an infant, then drew us close on the cross, dying for all our rebellions, to restore us and all creation. I see and hear it all everywhere.

The Psalm 1 trail takes us to exultation too. The book of praises ends in psalms so exultant they nearly sweep us away with their force.

> Praise the LORD.
>   Praise the LORD, my soul.
> I will praise the LORD all my life;
>   I will sing praise to my God
>   as long as I live.[1]

And then the final verse of the final psalm of the entire Psalter ends,

> Let everything that breathes
>   sing praises to the LORD!
> Praise the LORD![2]

The gate of Psalm 1 told us of "the joys of those who . . . delight in the law of the LORD"[3]—and now in these final psalms we see and hear the fulfillment of that joy and delight. Look, listen! All creation, from God's people to the worm in the dirt to the creatures at the bottom of the sea and out into the infinitude of the cosmos—all are summoned to shout and sing exuberant praise to God.

These five final psalms (Psalms 146 to 150) are sometimes called the hallelujah psalms, as each one begins and ends with the exuberant call "Hallelujah!" *Hallelujah* is two Hebrew words—*hallelu* (from the root *halal,* translated in nearly all English versions of the Bible as "to praise") and *Yah* (the shortened form of the name Yahweh). The compound word is almost always translated "Praise the Lord." *Hallelu Yah!* is not itself the praise; it is a summons to praise. But a preeminent Hebrew scholar goes further, expanding the verb *halal* into "to celebrate hilariously, to be clamorously foolish, to rave, to make a show, to shine forth."[4] The verb *hallelu* is imperative and plural, so *hallelujah* means "You! Every one of you! Come give praise, honor, admiration to Yah! Rave! Make a show! Shine forth! Celebrate!"

The rapture of these psalms might shake and scare us right now. We might still be lingering in lament. We might be camped out in confession. Or still on our knees needing wisdom. These last few years, I've spent a lot of time in these places. Turning the page and arriving at these final hallelujahs doesn't mean our lives arrive here too.

Just after walking the long path toward forgiving my father before he died, I knew God was calling me to share that walk. I was reluctant and ran the other way, until I could run no longer. Two years later, when my book on forgiving my father released, a series of phone calls and emails from a beloved family member ensued, until the last one: "I never want to see you again." For weeks—months—I was lost in silent grief. The psalms, though, finally gave me words. Through them I have wailed and mourned; I have questioned, confessed, doubted. I even found entrance to some measure of gratitude. But praise has not come easily.

Still captive to grief, I need to move. I pack my bags and go in search of praise. I fly overseas and follow the journeys of Paul and the life of David. I need to do more than study these God-followers who praised even amid crises and fears. I want to understand this kind of praise with my whole being. How did David, running for his life from a man who was once a father to him, keep singing to God, "You are my strength, I sing praise to you"?[5] How did Paul, bloodied and shackled to a dungeon wall, sing praises so authentically and joyfully that the other prisoners gave their lives to this Jesus he was singing about? I sit in the stone tomb of Mamertine prison in Rome, where Paul was held just before he was martyred. I ride a raft out to the waters around Malta, where Paul was shipwrecked. I take a bus into the wilderness of Judea, where David hid from King Saul. I read the Psalms, the Epistles in these places, but the answer comes at the very end of my travels.

It's spring now, early April. This is my last Sunday before the trip ends. I am in a church in France, an English-speaking church of around a hundred people. We sit on children's wooden school chairs in a rented space, facing a cross made of twigs on the wall.

The sanctuary hums as people visit. An elderly woman, teenage boys, groups clustering around babies. I taught a seminar here yesterday and met many of them. I recognize the Nigerian woman with a newborn snuggled into her arms. The woman across the aisle is from South Africa. There's a family from Iran, another from Pakistan. I see the woman from Malaysia, the couple from Korea.

A worship leader approaches a music stand up front. We rise and read Psalm 150 together, all the accents and timbres blending into one:

¹Praise the LORD!

Praise God in his sanctuary;
   praise him in his mighty heaven!
²Praise him for his mighty works;
   praise his unequaled greatness!
³Praise him with a blast of the ram's horn;
   praise him with the lyre and harp!
⁴Praise him with the tambourine and dancing;
   praise him with strings and flutes!
⁵Praise him with a clash of cymbals;
   praise him with loud clanging cymbals.
⁶Let everything that breathes sing praises to the LORD!

Praise the LORD![6]

We remain standing. We sing now, with a keyboard and
a guitar.

How great is our God, sing with me
How great is our God, and all will see
How great, how great is our God[7]

My hands lift, reaching. I see old hands near mine.
Children's hands. A baby cries. A child whines. Our voices
swell. I have heard some of their stories. One woman, preg-
nant, walked across a mountain range to get here, fleeing for
her life. The woman on my left, from a Muslim background,

was abandoned by her husband, left alone to raise her children. Through a Bible study she came to Jesus. I stand here singing, bearing my own burdens.

A man in jeans and a crisp white shirt and a woman wrapped in a colorful African scarf step to the podium now. The woman reads in a clear voice:

> He went and took the scroll from the right hand of him who sat on the throne. And when he had taken it, the four living creatures and the twenty-four elders fell down before the Lamb. Each one had a harp and they were holding golden bowls full of incense, which are the prayers of God's people. And they sang a new song, saying:

> "You are worthy to take the scroll
>> and to open its seals,
> because you were slain,
>> and with your blood you purchased for God
>> persons from every tribe and language and people
>>> and nation.
> You have made them to be a kingdom and priests to
>> serve our God,
>> and they will reign on the earth."[8]

The man reads:

> He who was seated on the throne said, "I am making everything new!" . . . He said to me: "It is done. I am the

Alpha and the Omega, the Beginning and the End. To the
thirsty I will give water without cost from the spring of the
water of life. Those who are victorious will inherit all this,
and I will be their God and they will be my children.[9]

I cannot contain my wonder. On the last Sunday of my
trek, God has led me here, among these people who have
journeyed great distances, across mountains, deserts, and
seas, from mosques and synagogues, from far countries and
nearby neighborhoods. People who have fled for their lives,
people rejected by their families because of Jesus. People of
every color and tongue who have followed Jesus. They have
come through hard, long paths to these moments of praise.
Here we are together abandoning our pride, our defenses,
our fears, our losses, our griefs to stand face-to-face before
one another and before Yahweh's throne. Here is my King
and my Father. Here is my family. We are each other's fathers
and mothers, sisters and brothers. Mourning is turning to
dancing. I want to sing forever. Now I know that I shall. That
we all will. Because this is where and how the Psalm 1 path
ends. All the twists and turns of our stories—David's, the
Israelites', Paul's, mine—will bring us here before the throne.
God is here. We are exiles no longer. We are home.

But I have another home too. The next day I pack my
bags and fly back to Alaska, to my husband, to my work,
to long calls with my children and grandchildren, to the
coming fishing season. I am not disappointed. I know that
in this life, these moments of communal joy in the coming

city of God are fleeting. And I know, too, that I will not dwell in the hallelujah psalms every day. Because next week, maybe even tomorrow, I will need lament. And as I prepare for the upcoming fishing season, I will need a lot of wisdom. I will always need prayers of confession and trust. I look forward to rich moments of worship in creation and times of thanksgiving. I know I need them all. And my Father knows too.

That day in the country church when I raised my hand to grab hold of Jesus, I could not believe the good news I had just heard. That God is not distant, that he is relational, intentional, pursuing a people for himself—a people to love, to nurture, to be his children. The Son came down, he came close. He came all the way to the manger, all the way to the cross. And then, risen from death, all the way to our hearts. He came to dwell within us, within you, me. To bring us back to his Father and ours. No matter how far we might feel from our Father, he is closer than our next breath. He cannot come any nearer.

As we respond, we're joining a worldwide celebration. It's raucous. It's comprehensive, including the voices of everything that breathes and moves. God doesn't need this symphony. Our God is all-sufficient, complete, perfect, needing nothing, but even his invitations and commands to praise are for our good. Praise aligns our words, our minds, our hearts, our bodies with the very grain and groove of God's universe. Our voices join a choir that stretches beyond time, and as we lift our whole selves to our Father, he meets us there, in our worship. As we draw near to God, he draws near to us.[10]

We are invited there now, today—and one day, far off and soon, he will gather his family before his throne, to the garden, to the "river whose streams make glad the city of God."[11] This holy, joyous communion will not end! How can we not rejoice?

■ draw near

If our tongues are tight or tied, as mine often is, the hallelujah psalms give us a hundred reasons to shift our feet, to lift our eyes toward praise. Praise for God's mighty acts of creation. For his mercies in rescuing a stubborn people. Because he keeps his promises, even when we do not. Because his love never ends, though ours comes and goes. Because his judgments are always perfect and righteous. Because he has compassion on all his creation.

But we're prone to forget some of this, sometimes all of it. One of our biggest obstacles to praise can be our own busyness and distraction.

Our Father knows this about us. Just before the Hebrews set foot in their abundant new land, God cautioned them that their prosperity could make them proud and cause them to forget the Lord their God. To guard against such forgetting, he urges them, "When you have eaten and are satisfied, praise the LORD your God for the good land he has given you. Be careful that you do not forget the LORD your God."[12]

When we forget God, our reality changes. Our Father is still there, but we're not looking or listening. We're living removed from his presence. So we are stopping to remember, to look up and look around, to praise and celebrate our God-with-us. In our practice, we're going to dig into Psalm 145. Before we do, let's remember our acronym for entering into prayer through the Psalms:

NEARING

- **N**otate (Write out the original psalm by hand, an action that uses both sides of the brain.)
- **E**xpress (Use your voice and body gestures/movements to give full expression to the psalm.)
- **A**mplify (Add your response/circumstance/witness to the psalm.)
- **R**ead (Understand the original psalm in its context, reading different versions if desired.)
- **I**dentify (Personalize the psalm to you and/or to your faith community.)
- **N**ew Testament Fulfillment (Add relevant New Testament verses that augment and fulfill the message of the psalm.)
- **G**ather (Share psalm-prayers in worship with your faith community.)

We will enter these words and allow them to draw us nearer to the heart of God in praise: **Express, Read, Notate, New Testament Fulfillment,** and **Amplify**.

Express

Praise is a verb, an action! While we usually read and write into the psalms first, then allow those words to guide our physical expression and worship of God, we're going to start differently with praise. Neuroscientists are discovering that emotions often follow our muscles, not vice versa. Our physical movements and expressions, from large muscles to small, have a profound effect on our thinking, our feeling, and our whole sense of well-being. Didn't God tell us to love him with all our heart, soul, mind, and strength?

King David gives us a dramatic image of whole-body worship. When the Ark of the Lord, representing the presence of God, was brought to Jerusalem, David "danced before the LORD with all his might," accompanied by "shouts of joy and the blowing of rams' horns."[13]

1. As you reread the praise psalms in this chapter, choose one that resonates in your spirit. Don't worry if you feel distant from the words at the start. Just be willing to begin. Start by reading it aloud. As you read, lift your arms, reaching for God. As you speak out the attributes of God, use your arms and hands to punctuate each attribute with a physical expression of affirmation and joy. Allow your body to become the instrument of praise.

2. Put on some upbeat praise music that brings a smile to your face and heart. Dare to dance! Allow yourself to be

clamorously foolish and boisterous. Let joy pour in and out of you. Release your body to find its full expression of praise and gratitude to God.

3. In Psalm 9:1 David writes, "I will praise you, LORD, with all my heart." Psalm 146 opens exultantly with "Let all that I am praise the LORD." As you offer praise back to God through these psalms, what gifts and talents has he given uniquely to you that you could offer back in praise?

Read and Notate

Reflecting on the hallelujah psalms in this chapter, consider the varied ways God's people and God's creation offer praise.

1. **Read** Psalm 145 all the way through. It's a compendium of different forms and expressions of praise presented as an acrostic with twenty-two lines, each line beginning with a successive letter of the Hebrew alphabet. Like Psalm 119, this connotes completion. We understand the message: Despite life's alphabet of loss, from A to Z no one is more worthy of our praise than Yahweh.

Psalm 145

A PSALM OF PRAISE OF DAVID.

¹ I will exalt you, my God and King,
   and praise your name forever and ever.
² I will praise you every day;
   yes, I will praise you forever.

³ Great is the LORD! He is most worthy of praise!
No one can measure his greatness.

⁴ Let each generation tell its children of your mighty acts;
let them proclaim your power.
⁵ I will meditate on your majestic, glorious splendor
and your wonderful miracles.
⁶ Your awe-inspiring deeds will be on every tongue;
I will proclaim your greatness.
⁷ Everyone will share the story of your wonderful
goodness;
they will sing with joy about your righteousness.

⁸ The LORD is merciful and compassionate,
slow to get angry and filled with unfailing love.
⁹ The LORD is good to everyone.
He showers compassion on all his creation.
¹⁰ All of your works will thank you, LORD,
and your faithful followers will praise you.
¹¹ They will speak of the glory of your kingdom;
they will give examples of your power.
¹² They will tell about your mighty deeds
and about the majesty and glory of your reign.
¹³ For your kingdom is an everlasting kingdom.
You rule throughout all generations.

The LORD always keeps his promises;
he is gracious in all he does.

¹⁴ The LORD helps the fallen
and lifts those bent beneath their loads.
¹⁵ The eyes of all look to you in hope;
you give them their food as they need it.
¹⁶ When you open your hand,
you satisfy the hunger and thirst of every
living thing.
¹⁷ The LORD is righteous in everything he does;
he is filled with kindness.
¹⁸ The LORD is close to all who call on him,
yes, to all who call on him in truth.
¹⁹ He grants the desires of those who fear him;
he hears their cries for help and rescues them.
²⁰ The LORD protects all those who love him,
but he destroys the wicked.

²¹ I will praise the LORD,
and may everyone on earth
bless his holy name
forever and ever.

2. **Notate** the psalm, writing it out by hand. Consider playing instrumental music in the background as you do.

New Testament Fulfillment

Praise is not the concern only of the Psalms. The New Testament echoes the message of these songs: that praise is the heart of our created purpose. Before you begin, consider one or several of these New Testament passages to add to your psalm-prayer as you continue, further opening your eyes and tongue to praise:

> In Him also we have obtained an inheritance, being predestined according to the purpose of Him who works all things according to the counsel of His will, that we who first trusted in Christ should be to the praise of His glory.[14]

> But you are a chosen generation, a royal priesthood, a holy nation, His own special people, that you may proclaim the praises of Him who called you out of darkness into His marvelous light.[15]

> Therefore by Him let us continually offer the sacrifice of praise to God, that is, the fruit of our lips, giving thanks to His name.[16]

Amplify

1. Psalm 145 contains several entry points to **Amplify**, adding your own voice and story. Consider each of these as you begin to weave together your psalm-prayer:

   - Verse 4: Tell your children of his mighty acts in your life.

   - Verses 5-6: What miracles and awe-inspiring deeds has God done in your life?

- Verse 13: How has God kept his promises to you?

- Verse 14: How has he helped you when you've fallen?

- Verse 19: How has he granted your desires?

- Verse 20: How has he protected you?

2. If you'd like more of a challenge, try to parallel David's acrostic form in this psalm, beginning each verse with a successive letter of the alphabet. Yes, this will take more time, but I assure you, the extra intentionality as you consider the goodness of God will be deeply rewarding!

Praise Psalms[17]

While most psalms include elements of praise, these are the psalms focused primarily on offering praise to Yahweh.

Psalms 8, 29, 33, 46–48, 65, 67, 68, 76, 81, 84, 85, 92, 95–100, 103, 108, 111–115, 117, 135, 136, 145–150

a new song

When I was twelve, I lied to get into a movie. I was with my best friend, Debbie. I had a dollar in my pocket, all my money in the world. I had been to one other movie in my life. I could hardly contain my excitement.

But the twelve-and-over admission fee was two dollars. I did the only thing I could think of: I said I was eleven and, with a quavering hand and queasy stomach, handed all my worldly cash to the ticket taker. In the dark of the theater, I was soon swept away into history, into the desert, enthralled by the epic playing out before me. Until the robed and white-bearded man climbed a mountain and spoke with God at the fiery summit.

I was looking for God, and there he was. But then I realized: I had lied to get into *The Ten Commandments*. I wanted to reach out my hand to the top of that blazing mountain, but I had lied. Clearly I was guilty and God was unreachable.

Many years later I stand on a beach in Kodiak, Alaska,

with twenty-two others, my arms raised to the orange skies. The mountains glow pink. It's nearly eleven o'clock at night, and the sun has not set yet. It's the last night of our week together, a time of writing and praying through the Psalms. People have traveled thousands of miles to be here. We've cooked kebabs over the campfire on the beach, and now before dinner we hold the psalm-prayers we wrote. We read Psalm 34 together, a psalm of praise and rescue. The surf foams behind us. Humpbacks breach on the horizon. When we come to verse 4—

I sought the LORD, and he answered me;
   he delivered me from all my fears[1]

—we each read out from our own prayers the ways he has delivered us. We are a joyful choir of rescues. And we know we are heard, that our Father is here among us.

After, Judy Mandeville leads us in a Hebrew praise dance. We are not dancers, and we laugh at our awkwardness. We've come from faraway places, from dirt roads, through wilderness wanderings. All of us carrying secrets, failures, and wounds. But God came after us, one by one. He came down off the mountain. He came near. He spoke to us. Through his Word. Through Jesus. He placed us in a family beyond borders. He spoke, and he wants us to answer back. We're doing it. We're learning to "sing a new song"[2] to our Father from wherever we are on the path.

None of our songs—not mine, not those on the beach,

not yours today—are lost. None of our prayers are hidden. Our songs, our movements, everything offered in prayer—all are held in our Father's hands. Our peek into heaven through the book of Revelation shows us bowls of incense near God's throne: "the prayers of God's people."[3]

I keep my prayers as well, mostly in journals. I have a stack of these journals now, and I come back to them again and again. Often I read them in tears. Each prayer forges a way through silence and the fractures of the world, returning to and beholding the reign of Yahweh over my life and my being, over all things. I see now all the ways God has answered these prayers.

Thank you for joining me in these pages, for adding your voice to mine and to those of our sisters and brothers. It is no small thing to bring your words to the page and to prayer, to reach out to find the God who can seem far but—I pray you will find—is very near. Someday, I know, we'll sing our new songs together. We'll be side by side with each other and face-to-face with our Father.

Let's get ready for that day.

notes

INTRODUCTION

1. Psalm 10:1, NIV.
2. Psalm 44:24, ESV.
3. Psalm 22:1, NRSV.
4. Psalm 13:1, NIV.
5. Psalm 73:14.
6. Psalm 6:4, BSB.
7. Psalm 51:1-2.
8. Psalm 23:1, NKJV.
9. Psalm 46:1, ESV.
10. Psalm 40:2.
11. Psalm 55:22, ESV.
12. Psalm 23:2, ESV.
13. Psalm 77:1, NIV.
14. Psalm 119:105, MSG.
15. Psalm 28:1.
16. Psalm 86:12, NIV.
17. Psalm 5:1, ESV.
18. Psalm 13:1-2, HCSB.
19. Neurotheology connects neurology (how the brain functions and how we learn) with spiritual formation.
20. Jim Wilder and Michel Hendricks, *The Other Half of Church: Christian Community, Brain Science, and Overcoming Spiritual Stagnation* (Chicago: Moody Publishers, 2020), 25.
21. Quoted in K. J. Ramsey, "The Best Way to Memorize Scripture Has Little to Do with Learning Words," *Christianity Today*, September 21, 2020, https://www.christianitytoday.com/ct/2020/october/science-scripture-memorization-heart-head-knowledge.html.

22. Mark 12:30.
23. Psalm 33:3, 40:3, 96:1, 98:1, 144:9, and 149:1.
24. 1 Samuel 13:14.

CHAPTER ONE | ENTERING THROUGH THE OPEN GATE

1. Joshua 1:7-8, NIV.
2. Gordon J. Wenham, *Psalms as Torah: Reading Biblical Song Ethically*, (Grand Rapids, MI: Baker Academic, 2012), 7.
3. Psalm 119:32, WEB.
4. Included with Heidi's permission.
5. See Anne Mangen and Jean-Luc Velay, "Digitizing Literacy: Reflections on the Haptics of Writing," in *Advances in Haptics*, ed. Mehrdad Hosseini Zadeh (Intech, 2010), https://doi.org/10.5772/8710. See also Sreelakshmi S. Kumar and Bhagyajyoti Priyadarshini, "Hand and Pen: A Match Made in Heaven," Project Encephalon and The Science Paradox, https://www.projectencephalon.org/post/hand-and-pen-a-match-made-in-heaven.

CHAPTER TWO | CRYING OUT IN LAMENT

1. Psalm 2:1-3, NIV.
2. Psalm 3:1-2, NIV.
3. Psalm 4:1, NIV.
4. Psalm 5:1-2, NIV.
5. Psalm 6:2-3, NIV.
6. Hosea 11:8, ESV.
7. Matthew 23:37-38.
8. Matthew 27:46, NIV.
9. Psalm 32:3, NIV.
10. Psalm 3:8.
11. Psalm 4:8.
12. Psalm 5:11-12.
13. Psalm 6:9, NIV.
14. Hebrews 12:2, CEB.
15. "Psychiatrist Explains How the Brain Blocks Memory to Help Get through Traumatic Event," News Medical, December 9, 2016, https://www.news-medical.net/news/20161209/psychiatrist-explains-how-the-brain-blocks-memory-to-help-get-through-traumatic-event.aspx.
16. Romans 8:39, ESV.
17. Ephesians 6:10-12, NIV.
18. Matthew 5:44.

19. Included with Jenn's permission.
20. See Hermann Gunkel, *Introduction to Psalms: The Genres of the Religious Lyric of Israel* (Macon, GA: Mercer University Press, 1998).

CHAPTER THREE | ASKING FOR WISDOM

1. Charlotte Elliott, "Just as I Am," 1835, public domain.
2. Psalm 119:1-2, HCSB.
3. Psalm 119:4-5, NIV.
4. Psalm 119:19, HCSB.
5. Psalm 119:29.
6. Psalm 119:73.
7. Psalm 119:84.
8. Psalm 119:154.
9. Deuteronomy 4:5-7, HCSB (emphasis added).
10. Psalm 119:176.
11. James 1:5, ESV.
12. See Hermann Gunkel, *Introduction to Psalms: The Genres of the Religious Lyric of Israel* (Macon, GA: Mercer University Press, 1998) and David Witthoff, Kristopher A. Lyle, Matt Nerdahl, and Eli Evans, *Psalms Explorer* (Faithlife, 2014), https://www.logos.com/product/45685/psalms-explorer.
13. Psalm 119:174.

CHAPTER FOUR | RESTING IN TRUST

1. Psalm 121:5-8, NIV.
2. See Exodus 34:6-7, NIV. The NIV translates *hesed* as "love" in this verse.
3. Psalm 23:1-3, NIV.
4. Psalm 22:12.
5. Psalm 22:13.
6. Psalm 18:2.
7. Psalm 3:3.
8. Psalm 121:5.
9. Psalm 34:8, NIV.
10. See Hermann Gunkel, *Introduction to Psalms: The Genres of the Religious Lyric of Israel* (Macon, GA: Mercer University Press, 1998).

CHAPTER FIVE | BEING HONEST IN CONFESSION

1. 1 Samuel 13:14.
2. Romans 7:15, NIV.

3. Gordon J. Wenham, *Psalms as Torah: Reading Biblical Song Ethically* (Grand Rapids, MI: Baker Academic, 2012), 52.
4. Psalm 106:1-5.
5. Psalm 106:16-39.
6. Genesis 3:15.
7. Psalm 51:1, ESV.
8. Psalm 32:1-2, NIV.
9. Psalm 103:11-14, NIV.
10. Psalm 27:10.
11. Included with Tyler's permission, Jeremiah 20:9, NIV.
12. Psalm 51:10, KJV.
13. Psalm 51:1-3, ESV.
14. Psalm 32:10.
15. 1 John 1:9, NIV.
16. 2 Corinthians 7:10, NIV.
17. 2 Peter 3:9, NIV.
18. Romans 2:4, NIV.
19. Joshua Rabin, "Physical Movement in Jewish Prayer," My Jewish Learning, https://www.myjewishlearning.com/article/physical-movement-in-jewish-prayer.
20. See *Psalms* (Colorado Springs: NavPress, 2010).

CHAPTER SIX | BEHOLDING CREATION

1. Psalm 8:1, NIV.
2. Psalm 19:1-2, ESV.
3. Psalm 104:17-18.
4. Psalm 104:1-4, YLT.
5. Psalm 104:13-15, YLT.
6. Psalm 139:13-15, NKJV.
7. Psalm 33:5, NIV.
8. Ephesians 2:10, NKJV.
9. Included with Naomi's permission.
10. Genesis 1:31.
11. See Robert McCabe, "The Genre of the Psalms," Detroit Baptist Theological Seminary (blog), July 22, 2012, https://dbts.edu/2012/07/22/the-genre-of-the-psalms.

CHAPTER SEVEN | REJOICING IN THANKSGIVING

1. Psalm 107:1-2, NIV.
2. Psalm 107:8, 15, 21, 31, NIV.

3. Psalm 28:6-7, ESV.
4. Psalm 116:1-2, NIV.
5. Deuteronomy 4:9, HCSB.
6. Psalm 107:21-22, NIV.
7. Ephesians 2:13, NIV.
8. Psalm 107:3, NIV.
9. Revelation 7:9.
10. See Hermann Gunkel, *Introduction to Psalms: The Genres of the Religious Lyric of Israel* (Macon, GA: Mercer University Press, 1998).

CHAPTER EIGHT | OFFERING PRAISE

1. Psalm 146:1-2, NIV.
2. Psalm 150:6.
3. Psalm 1:1-2.
4. James Strong, *Strong's Expanded Exhaustive Concordance of the Bible* (Nashville: Thomas Nelson, 2009), s.v. "הָלַל."
5. Psalm 59:17, NIV.
6. Psalm 150.
7. Chris Tomlin, "How Great Is Our God," *Arriving*, sixsteps/Sparrow, 2004.
8. Revelation 5:7-10, NIV.
9. Revelation 21:5-7, NIV.
10. James 4:8, ESV.
11. Psalm 46:4, NIV.
12. Deuteronomy 8:10-11, NIV.
13. 2 Samuel 6:14-15.
14. Ephesians 1:11-12, NKJV.
15. 1 Peter 2:9, NKJV.
16. Hebrews 13:15, NKJV.
17. See David Witthoff, Kristopher A. Lyle, Matt Nerdahl, and Eli Evans, *Psalms Explorer* (Faithlife, 2014), https://www.logos.com/product/45685/psalms-explorer.

EPILOGUE | A NEW SONG

1. Psalm 34:4, NIV.
2. Psalm 98:1.
3. Revelation 5:8.

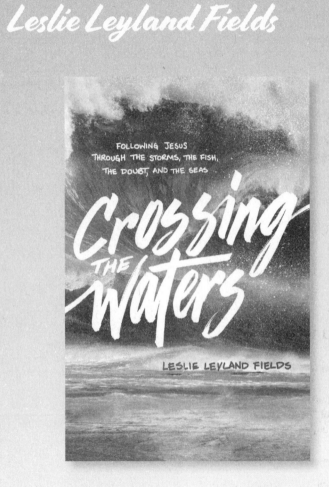

Harvester Island Writers' Workshop

Off the coast of Kodiak, Alaska

Harvester Island is a wild, stunningly beautiful place for retreat, growth, community, and workshops

Guest writers have included Ann Voskamp, Philip Yancey, Luci Shaw, Bret Lott, Jeanne Murray Walker, Scot McKnight, Paul Willis, and Marilyn MacEntyre

LESLIE LEYLAND FIELDS
leslieleylandfields.com

"Seeing the group photo with the stunning views of Harvester Island brought tears to my eyes. These were tears of joy and deep gratitude for the time we had together in such a phenomenal setting with joy-filled hospitality and unparalleled teaching of your craft. I bask in the delight in making friends who love words and writing. I am a beginner, honored to have been there with you all!" — Clydette

CP1171

EXPERIENCE YOUR STORY
FOR GOD'S GLORY

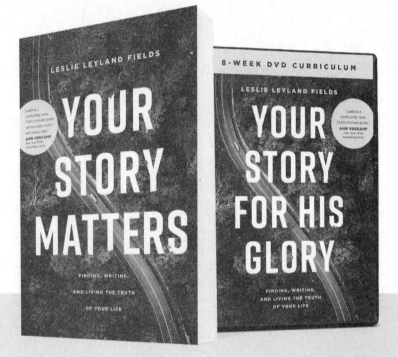

Read *Your Story Matters* together with the companion eight-week video curriculum available on RightNow Media. Leslie Leyland Fields invites you to her Alaskan writing retreat to explore a dynamic writing process with Ann Voskamp and twenty other writers. You'll soon be writing from your own life, discovering new spiritual truths, reclaiming the past, sharing hope, and passing on your own extraordinary legacy.

Great for group or personal use.